HER BIG IDEA

HER BIG IDEA

THE NEXT GENERATION
OF FEMALE ENTREPRENEURS

HALEY HOFFMAN SMITH

NEW DEGREE PRESS

HER BIG IDEA

The Next Generation of Female Entrepreneurs

ISBN   978-1-64137-110-0   *Paperback*

ISBN   978-1-64137-111-7   *Ebook*

To my Mom,
who nurtured and supported every one of my BIG ideas.

CONTENTS

*So this, I believe, is the central question
upon which all creative living hinges:
Do you have the courage to bring forth the
treasures that are hidden within you?*

—ELIZABETH GILBERT,
BIG MAGIC: CREATIVE LIVING BEYOND FEAR

INTRODUCTION

"I think you're screwing me over," read her email. "You're a hypocrite and I don't trust you."

This, and a slew of other concerns, compiled the novel-length email that arrived in my inbox one sunny June morning. As I read and re-read the words libelously lambasting my character, rage boiled inside of me—probably exacerbated by the steaming cup of coffee in my hand. I was at the local Pancake House, which is hardly the place to receive an email like this. But alas.

She pulled no punches, which given the prior six months of our strained business partnership, shouldn't have surprised me. But I was surprised—surprised that she could create such an inaccurate vision of me, met with such anger. Then, a deeper feeling of shame welled up. I had been so naïve.

I was only twenty when we had started our business venture together. She was twice my age with a perceived wealth of financial experience, and I was the creative visionary. We were the perfect pair. Our relationship was initially a walk in the park, as all cofounder relationships are in their sunny beginnings, otherwise known as the "honeymoon phase." We had worked together in harmony on my first nonprofit, spent days laughing and collaborating in coffee shops and over meals, and this new venture rose as a natural ancillary. We both thought there was a business opportunity with the new company, an opportunity and idea that was not only fulfilling, but could be quite lucrative.

Yet as we progressed from the idea stage—when it was fun to imagine, dream and hope—into the "let's get this show on the road" stage, it became clear that "partnership" is just a well-intentioned word spoken at the beginning of a venture that quickly loses its meaning as daily operations play out. We shook across the table equity wise, fifty-fifty, my half ownership from my sweat equity to date (the work I had done before the company formed) and hers from her financial investment. She had offered to put her personal funds to work for our venture, which would include website development, the merchandise, and a launch party. These were some of the most exciting moments of my life; we understood each other on a creative level, and everything we touched, from the apparel to the launch party, turned to magic.

A few weeks after our launch party, she left the country to travel, saying she could run the company from afar. We had every intention to make the new arrangement work, but inevitably, the distance and the abrupt halt to the productivity killed our momentum. I should have seen the red flag here, because it was a-wavin', but my all-too-trusting nature pushed aside any anxieties.

I naturally felt uneasy about the money in the venture being hers; money almost always creates an implicit power dynamic.

Ah, yes. *Money.* Cash is king in a new venture, and I had no idea where we stood.

"Could I see the latest financials?" or "I still don't have access to the bank statements," I would ask.

She would reply that she would pull it together later.

I was tasked with writing the business plan, but an author needs a deep understanding of the *financials* to write a compelling one. Six months into the venture, I had yet to see a single number about our business.

I learned that once communication went out the window, there was no hope for recovery. It was impossible to communicate because of the spotty service abroad. I couldn't shake the feeling that I felt like an intern in my own company while she admitted she pushed her own to-do list to the side. When I suggested a strategic business decision to gain back the momentum we lost after the launch party, she said:

"Whoever has the money calls the shots."

Gut punch.

I felt I lost my autonomy over the one thing I had created in my life.

And, I had a lost a friend, too. Someone I cared deeply for, and truly believed I would be in business with forever.

This email was the call to an end.

After all I had done and sacrificed and given—all that I *could* give at twenty years old.

I was totally and absolutely dumbfounded.

I was *done*.

But here's the real insight from that email. I wasn't done with following my dreams, working on my passions or running after something I believed in.

I had a lot to learn, and I had to get back up again. And I would.

Researchers Sheryl Ball, Catherine C Eckel, and Maria Heracleous found that women are perceived to be more risk averse than men.[1] In fact, over the past few decades, countless studies have concluded that men are just more likely to take risks than women.

Perhaps the bigger issue with this is that the implications of these findings show that women are at a distinct disadvantage when it comes to getting support for risk taking.

"Just be careful," I'd often hear from friends and advisors. "Starting something like this is risky—did you know that 90 percent of startups fail?"

This "be careful" attitude is ingrained in women early in life.

In a study published in the *Journal of Pediatric Psychology* in 2016, Elizabeth O'Neal, Jodie Plumert, and Carole Peterson found that parents are "four times more likely to tell girls than boys to be more careful" after mishaps that are not life-threatening but do entail a trip to the emergency room.[2]

I'm certainly not saying we should encourage our kids to totally throw caution into the wind and fly off the monkey bars without a parachute, but there is a perception created that girls are more fragile than boys.

O'Neal, Plumert, and Peterson found that "girls may be less likely than boys to try challenging physical activities, which are important for developing new skills," because of this risk-averse attitude.

Another study in the *Journal of Applied Developmental Psychology* observed how parents engaged with their children at the playground. They found that parents cautioned their daughters about the dangers of the fire pole significantly more than they did their sons and were much more likely to assist them. On the other hand, both fathers and mothers instructed their sons to face their fears and offered advice, guidance and instruction on how to complete the obstacle without help.[3]

Well, I had seen the risky side all right. After taking a four-week breather from her and the company for an innovation program in Italy, I decided, finally, that I had too bright of a future to continue investing my time in a company doomed to fail. I knew I deserved and wanted a chance to create something new—something entirely my own—and execute it on my own terms.

It appeared from a public front to fizzle out quietly, but behind closed doors, it got ugly.

There were some questions: "Hey, whatever happened to that apparel you were selling?" or, "I've seen that sticker on your laptop around campus, where can I get one?" But for the most part, I pushed the experience down deep, where no one could learn about how it really ended. The truth is, I began to feel that despite studying business and loving creating ventures, the risk of entrepreneurship was just too great. I clearly didn't have the instincts to sniff out who I should and shouldn't go into business with.

One day, I was interviewing a visiting mentor for my thesis on women's self-agency in entrepreneurship and had finished asking all my questions. We still had a bit of time. Maybe it was her soothing voice, her calm presence, or the way she looked at me with a gentle knowing, but I felt compelled for the first time to share everything that had happened—with a complete stranger.

I shared my story, which hung thickly in the air as I took a deep breath, relieved to finally let the dragon out.

She stared back at me with awe.

"Haley, it seems that you have been really hurt by all has transpired."

I couldn't help it. My eyes filled with tears, and I felt the world I was carrying on my shoulders collapse.

She nodded knowingly as I quickly tried to wipe the tears overflowing in my eyes, and she continued, "It's impacted your ability to see yourself as the powerful woman you are."

She was right. I believed that my perceived failure said something about me as a person and my ability to create something in this world. I believed it rendered me broken and incapable of being the strong and empowered entrepreneur I had worked so hard to become.

And even though in that moment this successful woman assured me I was strong and powerful, the doubt would soon come back. In fact, at various points in the journey to create this book, those same feelings of failure sometimes rendered me paralyzed in trying to write and share.

I know, intellectually, that I have enough research to fill a series of books on entrepreneurship advice and wisdom.

But, while trying to write about this deeply personal failure, I texted my professor and told him I felt totally unequipped.

"What if they think I'm not credible enough to write it because my first company failed?" I asked.

"You are going to HAVE to get over that dumb idea," he wrote. "Because the next Haley needs to hear she'll get over her failures too if she takes a risk or tries to do something important."

Over the past year, I have interviewed, researched and studied hundreds of successful women, compiling to enough stories to fill a series of books. The research began for my honors thesis at Brown, on how women develop their sense of self agency in entrepreneurship and venture capital. What I found, and the stories I heard, riveted me. I had to learn more and DO more with what I was discovering and piecing together.

I sought to understand how each entrepreneur I read about and interviewed had navigated the path of taking a risk worth taking to achieve something important to them. I have heard countless stories much like mine—of struggles, challenges, and failures—but I also have heard many more of support, growth, and achievement that have helped me to not only process my own shortfalls, but also to understand how every woman can achieve the big ideas inside of us.

What follows is a roadmap to find your big idea—your BIG IDEA. It's the seven key themes that may be general to anyone but are particularly customized to women who have grown up in a world where we're told to "be careful" on the playground or discouraged from taking the calculated risks we ultimately need to take. As much as it's a roadmap, it's also a guide to process the struggles and bumps along the journey, which we'll all face.

Big(her) Ideas
Identify your Inspiration
Gather Your Support System

Iterate
Do It
Expand and Explode
Again. . . yes, you do it again

We'll dive into each of these sections of the BIG IDEA framework in the book. And remember, this isn't about some risky, haphazard approach to living your life. It's about finding a fulfilling approach to standing out in today's work.

This doesn't mean starting just anything—but creating and going after BIG BIG BIG ideas that fundamentally change the way we live our lives, that improve the day-to-day of people like us and even people not like us, and that solve a problem crying out to be fixed. This means taking big risks and calling them adventures, thrusting ourselves into the uncomfortable and calling it comfortable, and creating something we believe in. But to do this, we have to fundamentally change the basis of what we believe is possible for ourselves, given our unique set of circumstances and resources that have brought us here.

Just as important as offering a detailed framework backed up by some of the top research in the world, this book is fun—and something anyone can pick up and enjoy. In the book you'll hear stories and insights that include:

- The craziest stories of how some of today's most beloved products were created
- Personal experiences from dozens of entrepreneurs who have put their hearts and souls into their ventures—for better or worse
- Tips, tricks, and inspiration to serve as a comprehensive guide for the days you feel stuck.

- And, perhaps most importantly, a blueprint of how you can (and, most importantly, WILL) start your BIG idea and bring it to life.

And then, well, everything else. What's accounted for, what isn't. Unpredictability is the only thing predictable in entrepreneurship. We all know that coming up with your big idea is just the beginning. Everything goes haywire the second that puppy is in development, when it hits the market, or when it needs to pivot. Creating a startup is like riding a bike, but everything is on fire, the last wheel just chucked itself off, and you realize it's not a bike, but an off road 4x4 that you never read the operating manual for.

And don't worry, it's okay if you have zilch in your head right now. You actually don't have to have the idea yet to become an entrepreneur. You have everything you need in your self-awareness, life experience, and knowledge to come up with an amazing idea. The only "secret sauce" you need is your own—because we aren't given ideas without the capacity to pursue them and bring them to life.

Whatever gift you have, whatever lights your fire, THAT is what the world deserves from you. We all have something unique to contribute, and the fact you picked up this book proves that you're ready to create something of your own to birth into this world. You are more than capable. Whatever idea comes to you, whether it's already there within you or not, is YOURS because you are the one to bring it to life.

Trust in that, and trust in yourself.

And trust in the BIG that's about to unfold.

CHAPTER 1

WHAT IS A BIG IDEA?

———

I specifically remember coming home and saying, 'Dad, Dad, I tried out for this or that and I was horrible,' and he would high-five me and say, 'Way to go.'

~ SARA BLAKELY

Sara Blakely was the daughter of an artist mother and an attorney father and was raised, much like I was, to recognize failure as a positive experience. She intended to follow in her father's footsteps with the practice of law, but her low LSAT score gave her reason to think law may not be her strong suit. Instead, she took a sales position with Danka.

Unfortunately, this meant going from door to door in the Sunshine State in the heat of summer, wearing dress

clothes—like pantyhose—and selling fax machines. Livin'
the dream. Blakely's ambition and work ethic helped her reach
the role of national sales trainer by age twenty-five, but she
already had another idea brewing. A BIG idea.

Blakely liked how pantyhose gave her hips and waist a firmer
feel and smoothed panty lines, but she hated the visible seams
across the toes and, obviously, the relentless heat. She began
experimenting by cutting the feet off her pantyhose and wearing the footless pair with slacks and sandals to a party. The
bottoms rolled up throughout the evening, but Blakeley knew
she was onto something. . . BIG.

Blakely moved to Atlanta and pursued her idea in the background over the next two years. She kept her job with Danka
and spent her savings of $5,000, continuing to develop her
product. She realized that she needed a patent to protect her
BIG idea, but she couldn't find a female patent attorney in
Georgia (imagine that), nor did she want to spend the minimum $3,000 for any other (ahem, male) patent attorney.

So instead, she bought a patent book from Barnes & Noble
and wrote her own.

Then, design in hand, Blakely approached a multitude of hosiery mill representatives in North Carolina. After a number of vetoes from the men who led the hosiery industry, she returned to Atlanta.

She said she must have heard the word "no" a thousand times.

And well, *yeah*. What in the world did those men know about pantyhose?

She was undaunted by the rejection, but she wasn't sure what her next step should be. Two weeks later, a mill operator from Asheboro, North Carolina, called to say that his daughters endorsed her idea and that he would too. He also mentioned he thought the idea was downright crazy until he mentioned it to his daughters who said something to the extent of, "Dad, that's actually *genius*."

Over the next year, Blakely worked on a prototype, testing it based on the opinions of her mother and friends, who had been in the dark on her big plans. In her research, she found that hosiery had been created using the same size waistband on the same size mannequin across the board. She decided to create a variety of waistband sizes to fit the diverse builds of *real* women. Once her patent application was submitted, she began to create the packaging. Rather than sticking with the neutral colors that were common at the time, she chose red. She also decided to incorporate various body types in the design, instead of the standard model used by other companies.

When it came time to choose a name, she knew the "k" sound was successful in many areas of product placement and settled on "Spanks." She adjusted for her research into names, which indicated that constructed names were more memorable and easier to trademark and switched the "ks" for "x." In 2000, she trademarked "Spanx" online.

Blakely modeled her own tights for hours a day to managers in local department stores, showing pictures to the buyers of just how much Spanx tightened things up. One day, at a meeting with Neiman Marcus, she felt she was losing the buyer's interest. So, she dug into her "lucky red backpack," pulled out the product, and whipped them on to prove just how great Spanx really looked. After that meeting, Spanx were sold at Neiman Marcus, Saks, Bergdorf Goodman, and Bloomingdales. Jackpot.

She also sent a gift basket to Oprah containing several of the products. Later that year, Oprah announced that Spanx were on her list of "Favorite Products," giving Spanx sales the boost Blakely needed to leave Danka and focus on her business, which had begun producing other garments like panties and bras.

And, well, that's how Blakely's initial perception of career failure post-LSAT and belief in her big idea landed her at the top of the richest self-made women list.

What is a BIG idea and how do you know you're onto one?

You may have an idea in your head about what BIG means now. You think of companies like AT&T, Google, Facebook— the sharks that ate the guppies, like Shutterfly acquiring Tiny Prints, or even the sharks that ate the sharks, like the recent acquisition of Whole Foods by Amazon.

For Sara, BIG meant she was willing to deal with sixty-one *NOs* to receive that one *YES* that would change her life.

My type of BIG idea means the following:

1. Blue
2. Intelligent
3. Grand

BLUE

Renée Mauborgne and W. Chan Kim authored a wildly successful book called *Blue Ocean Strategy: How to Create Uncontested Market Space and Make the Competition Irrelevant*, which presents a theory about business and ideation that turns the intention and goals of a company on their heads.[4]

When you come up with an idea and you're surveying the waters, one of the central questions is about competitors. Who are they, what do they have on you, and how can you surpass them?

The presence of competitors are what Mauborgne and Kim call a "bloody red ocean." There are sharks in the water, and the central intention of companies in this space is to outperform their rivals.

But the blue ocean is the new frontier. There are no competitors because it's an uncontested share of the market. You have free reign. You've created something so out of the ordinary, so new and BIG, that competitors aren't a concern.

Why compete when we can create?

~ RENÉE MAUBORGNE, CO-AUTHOR,
BLUE OCEAN STRATEGY

There's Netflix, which is rumored to have been created as a response to the fury over Blockbuster's high late fees and the convenience consumers want when they rent a movie. Netflix revolutionized the way in which we rent movies and consume entertainment. They thought of things like—hmm, maybe viewers want to watch an entire season of *Friends* in one sitting without having to wait for reruns on TV. Then, they took it further—"Hmm, maybe viewers don't need to hear the whole "Where You Lead" song at the intro of *Gilmore Girls* every time they start a new episode. Let's add a "skip intro" button." They anticipated users' needs and desires before we even had that idea in our head. Actually, they approached Blockbuster for a partnership, but Blockbuster couldn't figure out why they should be interested in this new product. I bet they regret that one.

There's Uber, which was created as a response to the annoyance of calling a cab and waiting forever for it to arrive or having to whistle for one in the streets of New York City, which didn't always go as seamlessly or seem as sexy as it did when Carrie Bradshaw did it in *Sex & The City*. They took that further, too, allowing us to share our rides with family members, to split the payment with other friends in the car and offering options like "Uber Pool" as a low-cost option. Of course, now, Lyft, in tandem with some recent company struggles, has turned Uber's ocean red.

These ideas have become so central to how we live our lives today (there have been so many days where I've both watched Netflix AND called an Uber) that we can't imagine life before them. But, before they came along, we couldn't imagine life with them, either. There was nothing out there quite like it. That's how they revolutionized the market as a whole.

They found their Blue Ocean.

These ideas also possess the two other nonnegotiables that comprise a BIG idea:

Intelligence—The founders had the intellectual capability to base these ideas on real customer needs and wants. Otherwise, we could create something totally wacky that few people want, just because it permits our entrance into a blue ocean.

Grandeur—Which is really what makes a BIG idea big. It's not always enough that an idea has no competitors in the space and was created intelligently. It has to have the intent to cover a scope of millions and billions of users, so much so that it gains a social importance that revolutionizes life as we know it now.

I'm fully well aware that the founders of both Netflix and Uber are men. You'll notice that all the other stories I'll share in this book are stories of female founders—many of them about truly BIG ideas—but the BIG BIG BIGGEST seem to be Netflix and Uber.

This bugged me a little bit. So, I sought to research why there's a discrepancy between the number of big ideas started by men and women.

While there's one school of thought that men and women are equal, I tend to think there's a slight nuance to that line of thinking.

Men and women are equal, but *different.*

One of the ways we are different is how we process a risky decision—perhaps deciding whether to pursue that BIG idea or not. Researchers Seda Ertac and Mehmet Gurdal found that the two largest factors we analyze when making a risky decision are:

1. the likelihood that the risk in question will help hit strategic objectives
2. the effect the risk will have on people involved.[5]

But here's where things get interesting. Author Doug Sundheim found that men put a stronger emphasis on the first risk whereas women put a stronger emphasis on the second in his book *Taking Smart Risks: How Sharp Leaders Win When Stakes Are High.*[6]

Risk is closely tied to intuition. We seldom take big risks unless we feel intuitively like it's going to go well. We don't really ignore that sick-to-our-stomach, "oh no this is bad" sensation when risk is involved.

Joel Pearson, an associate professor of psychology at the University of New South Wales in Australia, has studied our ability to tap into and harness that intuition and found in his research with Galang Lufityanto and Chris Donkin that "nonconscious emotional information can boost accuracy and confidence in a concurrent emotion-free decision task." We can train ourselves to better utilize our "gut" or our intuition in decision making over time.[7]

So, perhaps we can pursue the big ideas while trusting that we will intuitively avoid risk.

Standing where we are now, there's no way to truly know what revolutionary idea is going to shape the ordinary day our children live in or even the lives we live the next five to ten years. It's extremely difficult to imagine how an idea in our small heads could become a Blue, Intelligent, Grand Idea that people use every day—the type of idea that will become central to peoples' lives. That type of consideration is like an ant peering upward in the shadow of Mount Everest. Pursuing the BIG ideas oftentimes seems too much, too frightening, too downright impossible to even try.

But you aren't alone in that because no one knows how their idea will come to life and grow once it's out of their head and in the world.

Netflix founder Reed Hastings, upon striking his EUREKA! with his mail service DVD idea, purchased DVDs, shipped them to his friends and had them put the DVDs into the player to see if they still worked. He wanted to see if the operation was sustainable. Would DVDs get scratched? Would they break? Get lost in the mail? The whole mail service DVD idea was relatively simple. It was Blockbuster brought to Snail Mail, minus the fees. It was a variation on an already existing company, changed for convenience sake. It wasn't yet BIG, necessarily.

But the Netflix we know now is the giant that houses hundreds of TV shows and movies on a password-protected platform. The bold red letters give you access to the thousands of episodes that string together just to emotionally invest you in characters' lives, whereas before, you had to wait a week to watch the next episode or wait until it came on TV. The BIG idea plays out in smaller details—like that aforementioned ability to "skip recap" or "skip intro." It even plays out in creations of its own, with Netflix Original Series, like *Stranger Things*.

The point is: the BIG started with the small—all of the BIG ideas do. They have to. The natural evolution and the unfolding process of genius allows the small to grow and mold to become bigger. The key is to hold the vision. We can't constrain ourselves to small thinking and expect an idea to take on a life without the warmth of our hands and the creative genius in our noggins. That's our task.

You know when you're playing in the snow—the fluffy, powdery, perfectly sticky kind—and you start to make a snowball? At first, it fits in the palm of your hand and you pack more onto it, until it's so heavy you set it on the ground. You start to roll it and more snow sticks to it until it begins to grow in size as it gains more and more snow. Soon, you make three, and then you add the sticks, the carrots, the rocks, and you have a snowman. But it began with one small snowball.

It's the vision of the snowman that motivates the creation and the building. You don't need to slave away reaching the BIG idea. The minimally viable product is where that idea begins. Allow it to continue to grow and form and shape, and trust that an idea that you feel in your heart is worth pursuing is GOOD and worthy of growing even in its beginning stages.

A point I like to drive home is that numbers—statistics—don't lie. As of 2017, women comprise only 8 percent of the partners of the top one hundred venture capital firms.[8]

Also in 2017, when only 2 percent of venture capital went to female-founded companies, 79 percent of the venture capital spending went to *all male* teams.

And, when women *do* get funding, they raise an average of $77 million, whereas men raise an average of $100 million.[9]

This huge discrepancy puts a numerical value on the worth of female ideas and female-founded businesses—and the value is much lower than women deserve. First Round Capital analyzed its three hundred companies with six hundred founders over ten years and found that the teams with at least one female executive outperformed the all-male founder teams by 63 percent.[10]

If we know women are doing well with the capital they receive, why are they receiving less capital, if any at all?

These were the questions I set out to answer at the beginning of my senior year as I began my honors thesis on female self-agency in entrepreneurship and venture capital. A conversation with Scott Friend, the Managing Director of Bain Capital, was a pivotal moment in my research. Because he oversees the allocation of funding at one of the largest and most prestigious venture capital firms in the world, I wanted his opinion on why so few female-led companies are backed by venture funding. He sees all of the entrepreneurs that walk in the door, so I was hoping to understand if it was a matter of inequality on who was invited to pitch (as Bain's prestige necessitates quite a recommendation) or who was chosen for a deal.

Friend then said something that changed the course of my research. There is a disproportionate number of men over women who are *seeking funding in the first place*. When I asked why, he shared that women are often creating businesses that they run out of their homes in suburbia and that serve their local communities—businesses that simply do not need millions of dollars in venture backing. In other words, they aren't coming up with big ideas.

My question then became: why is it that women feel they cannot take up space in the business world and therefore create smaller ideas than men? What differentiates men and women in terms of the *size* of the business ideas they conjure? *What stops women from thinking BIG?*

As cited in *Growth-Oriented Women Entrepreneurs and Their Businesses: A Global Research Perspective* by Candida G. Brush, "women-led ventures were smaller than those of their male counterparts, whether measured by size of revenues generated or the number of people employed. . . the overarching question was: *Why do women-owned businesses remain smaller than those of their male counterparts?*"[11]

Barbara Tannenbaum teaches a famous class at Brown called Persuasive Communication, which helps her students become better public speakers. (Fun fact: the Founder of Airbnb went to the Rhode Island School of Design and was one of her students!)

She has an exercise in her staple talk that she gives at conferences or whenever she guest speaks. She asks everyone in the audience who identifies as female to sit like a male would, and vice versa—for the men to sit like women do.

All the women in the room *lounge*—legs and arms spread wide apart. We lean back into our seats and sprawl our limbs out as far as we can. I have to say, it's pretty comfortable.

The men sit up straight. They cross their legs. They cross their arms. They make themselves smaller.

She tells the room, "Women often feel like they should take up less space."

So, it seems pretty fitting that we can often make our *ideas* take up less space.

A few months ago, I had a conversation about an entrepreneurial idea of mine with the Associate Director at Brown's Nelson Center for Entrepreneurship. I was designing a wine label and wanted to talk through the details of how to license the label or sell it to wineries, so I was only in charge of the label itself.

He suggested a *bigger* version of my current idea—to buy the wine myself, own the inventory, slap my label on, and then take care of distribution and marketing myself. My first response was complete hesitation.

No way, I thought, could I ever *attempt* an idea that big. I just wanted to own a label, not a whole WINERY. It hadn't crossed my mind, and now that it had been presented to me,

I didn't think I was capable. He happened to be an empowering individual who did see my capacity for it. I immediately recognized that my hesitation was rooted in my limited self-agency as a female.

How was it that, after a semester of studying this very concern, I was still perpetuating the same limitations in my personal experience?

The bottom line is that we all constantly make up reasons why something can't be done.

This is just human nature. I don't believe we're natural pessimists (at least, not all of us). But, we're so paralyzed by the sense of the possible that we don't dare to dream about the impossible.

I think we can all relate to feeling, at times, like we're so small in the context of the world. How can something conjured in our own heads be BIG enough to make a ripple, let alone capture the world's attention?

This following story about the National Youth Orchestra in Iraq, which is a perfect example of Blue Ocean Strategy, proves that even when we feel small, we have the capacity to do BIG things.

In 2008, a seventeen-year-old girl in Iraq named Zuhul Satan wanted to start a national youth orchestra in Iraq. She tweeted this desire to the prime minister, and he responded by giving her $50,000 to fund her BIG idea and bring it to life.

(*Note to self: Just ASK. Say what you need to say—put your idea out there.*)

Paul McAlindin, a Scottish conductor, then met Zuhul, and wanted to help her start this orchestra.

But, he knew they lacked something. All the other national orchestras had millions of dollars in funding, had established themselves, and were more Western-world centric.

So, instead of starting an orchestra that was like all the others, they turned to purpose.

They turned to their blue ocean. They chose to create—to focus on their purpose—rather than to acquiesce to the red ocean competition.

Because of the conflict between the Sunnis and the Shiites in Iraq, the orchestra's mission became not only to make music, but to use music as a bridge to show the older generation that the new generation of Iraqis did not desire to fight like their parents.

They're now hailed as the "Bravest Orchestra in the World" by BBC.[12]

It all started with one desire.

One person.

One BIG idea.

CHAPTER 2

THE MYTH OF THE BIG IDEA

———

In 2006, Sophia Amoruso was a twenty-two-year-old campus safety officer in San Francisco with a limited sense of life direction but a knack for fashion.

Her favorite pastime was perusing the aisles of vintage stores, finding hidden gems that the owner of the store had underpriced and then purchasing and reselling them on eBay. She found that she had an unrecognized talent: to make another's 'trash' look like treasure, thanks to her styling skills, her models, and her photography.

I mean, when you can find a Chanel jacket on the back rack of a musty thrift store and turn that baby around for $1,000 of CHA CHING, you must be doing something right!

Imagine that magnificent sale—again, and again, and again. This girl was *talented*. She saw beyond what others could see when they looked at a lousy piece of clothing on a cheap hanger at the local Salvation Army and transformed it back to its former glory. And, she was a perfectionist. She made sure every label was arranged perfectly straight on the box and every dress was perfectly sewn and mended to the customers' desires. After building up her following on MySpace under the name "NastyGal" to over sixty thousand followers, she launched her own site—www.nastygal.com, bought a warehouse, moved into a headquarters in LA. By 2012, she had raised almost $50 million.

So, to say she accelerated *quickly* is an understatement. One day, she's broke and scrounging through the musty back aisles of San Franciscan vintage stores, and the next, she's turning a 900 percent profit in the comfort of her tiny apartment. She went on to raise $64 million and the company itself was valued at $85 million, landing her on the top of the *Forbes'* list of Richest Self-Made Women. The astronomical growth spurred the creation of her hit book and podcast #Girlboss (I recommend both) and a Netflix series of the same title based on her life and her rise to success.

It was the next big thing. Amoruso was at the height of her career—at the height of what most people hope and dream for in their careers—riding the buzz of the ecommerce boom with her keen eye for fashion sense and millennial style.

And then, the company went bankrupt.

The valuation of the company—which landed her at the top of that *Forbes'* Richest Self-Made Women list—went kapoot. Zilch. Zero.

Nasty Gal, originally worth $85 million, sold for a measly $20 million to a British competitor, Boohoo.com, and Amoruso was left with nothing. Oh yeah, and she got divorced in the midst of this.

It was called a riches-to-rags story, a total disaster. A fall from grace.

But Sophia Amoruso was one of the most quoted authors in my thesis. Her story, her experience, and her wisdom have altered my perception of entrepreneurship and who I can be as a #Girlboss more than so many of the entrepreneurs who "made it big" and, well, stayed big. Her story and her voice have inspired my colleagues, friends, and peers. So in the end, that's what I want to call big.

Why do we often measure size in dollars?

What is the impact if we do?

I was nearly one of those people—in fact, I too was enamored with the idea of venture capital, magazine covers in *Inc.* or *Fast Company* and the ego of Silicon Valley.

But, BIG doesn't mean a big pot of coins to swim in like Scrooge McDuck in *Duck Tails* (whoo hoo)! It doesn't mean 900 percent profit—even though hey, that's pretty nice, and I wouldn't turn it down.

BIG is really about impact.

My idea, despite its intention to be big, is also subject to circumstances and outside perception of it.

I started my first venture at age eighteen.

Lit without Limits was a nonprofit that aimed to impact girls globally via the unifying power of literature.

When I started it, I had no conception that I was an entrepreneur. I was taken aback when my aunt commended my "entrepreneurial spirit."

What, are you sure? Me?

I had just embarked on my first entrepreneurial venture, a nonprofit, but saw myself as more of a "director," and thought nonprofits were just organizations you start, none of that challenging entrepreneurship stuff necessary.

I had filed the forms to be a 501(c)3, recruited an advisory board, "hired" (pro-bono) staff members, and learned the ropes of running a nonprofit as I went along. This one moment of diving into uncharted territory based on a vision I had for how I could impact the world was the MOST influential learning experience of my life. I couldn't have learned any of what I've learned by reading. I had to do it, to experience it, and make adjustments to the company as I went along.

And it just happened that my idea, that had no intention of making any money, was big just for its intent: to get books into the hands of as many girls as I could, connecting a web of empowerment through literature internationally.

This was the same time in my life when I became friends with an entrepreneur a few years my senior, who had invented a nifty product for a specific consumer market. I learned much about business from him. He was assertive and didn't take no for an answer. He would find out a secretary's favorite flowers and send them to him or her to land a meeting with an investor. He would talk up everyone next to him on a plane, selling them his product right then and there. I really admired this about him.

He poured his knowledge into me: the right way to start networking, applications online I'd never heard of to track visitor data onto your website, and how to start my own blog to develop a personality brand. I soaked it in, took notes, rinsed and repeated.

I became more confident than ever during this period about the BIGness of my idea—just sharing its intention with others filled me to the brim with an enormous sense of purpose and direction. To me, the BIGness of my idea was not about how much money I was making (I was a nonprofit, after all), but rather how many women I could impact. I measured success by the testimonials of the girls in the program and by the reach of my mission. What I needed, to become truly "BIG" was press attention. This suspicion of mine was confirmed by many mentors and advisors I spoke with.

In my eyes, my idea would remain small until it had the platform to impact women at an international level.

Psychologists Kristen Elmore from Cornell University and Myra Luna-Lucero from Columbia University recently studied the light-bulb metaphor for how we come up with ideas and the gender biases about ideation processes. That magical "stroke of genius" moment when a light bulb goes off over the protagonist's head is associated with male ideation, whereas female ideation is likened to a seed that is nurtured to fruition over time.

Their study particularly focused on the perception of intelligence in response to the metaphors of the light bulb versus the seed and had surprising results. "For a female inventor, the seed (versus light bulb) metaphor increased perceptions of her genius, whereas the opposite pattern was observed for a male inventor," the researchers wrote.[13]

In other words, this moment of the big idea is romanticized more for men. Their genius is thought to "ding" like a light bulb and be big all at once, whereas for a woman, her moment of genius grows slowly—from the seed of an idea to its eventual BIGness, given the proper food, water, and sunlight.

My friend's "lightbulb" idea of his product seemed to get bigger by the day—in press attention and financials alike. He landed multiple TV appearances and his product was beginning to be featured in major national news publications. He paraded a piece of paper around that evaluated his company at over a million, proclaiming that it made HIM a millionaire, even though it was just a valuation. I remember scratching my head at that, questioning the veracity of that claim. How can one be a millionaire if the money isn't in your account? But, I was happy for him and celebrated along with him.

Meanwhile, I was chugging along, spending early mornings in coffee shops slurping the last sip of my Americano, desperately hoping for my lucky break. I'd send hundreds of cold emails to potential collaborators and was fixated on my inbox zero. Any progress I did make felt as slow as a seed growing to a sapling in the spring; it was growing, yes, but my idea was limited by its growth potential in the soil. I felt like I was a hamster running on its wheel, getting nowhere, losing breath.

Then, it began to occur to me that maybe all this BIG he was drumming up was...overinflated. I mentioned to someone close to him how wonderful it was that they had already been valued at $1 million. "Wow, that is VERY grandiose," she replied, completely surprised—and proving its falsehood.

Lightbulb sufficiently shattered.

When I asked him for some advice on gaining the same success in press and publications as he had gained, he shared that he spent $30,000 a month on a publicist who landed all this coverage for him. It became clear to me that his idea and his product was not necessarily gaining attention because of its merit. When press is involved, and top coverage can be achieved by investing the money in public relations, the allure and appear of the idea, product, and business certainly take on a bigger-than-life size.

This very understanding of big—based on company valuation—revealed itself to me as fallacious. Think back to Sophia Amoruso and NastyGal, and that valuation of $85 million. It wasn't her personal account that went bankrupt, and the valuation of NastyGal wasn't equivalent to its bank account, either.

Using valuation as a way to confer power as the CEO and/or founder of a company is similar to saying as a painter that your painting could be the next van Gogh, worth millions, and therefore you are a millionaire.

This very situation is not uncommon. Many founders are open about the valuation of their companies and invest their top dollar in publicity as a way of advertising their product. Don't get me wrong; this is totally fine. But, when you're just starting out as I was, it can seem that someone's idea or company is better or bigger than yours, when so much more is going on beneath the surface.

We have to remember that coming up with a big idea has to be big for its merit: How is your idea going to disrupt its industry, change the way your customers behave, and have a profound impact that spans states, countries, and groups of people? The value of an idea, and how big it is, is retained in that definition. I remember simply thinking that my nonprofit was so different from his product—and, perhaps, lesser. I thought I was so far behind, that I wasn't working hard enough.

How was it that with my heartfelt intentions and with what I wanted to do for girls internationally, my current progress so sharply contrasted from his? I knew I was working just as hard. I knew my heart was in the right place. And yet, I was totally and entirely stuck in place, on a hamster wheel, believing it had to be something wrong with **me**. In reality, I just wasn't over-projecting. I was being honest with the world and myself about how hard it can be to make progress in the entrepreneurial realm.

I'm a big fan of men and learn so much from them and have amazing relationships with men who are incredible business owners, but it's continuously brought to my attention how they tend to inflate their numbers and/or over-project some area of their business. I hear all the time—women are more COMPETENT. Men are more CONFIDENT. This is a massive disadvantage in the venture capital firm's office. The women are stating their projections that are rooted in reality and thorough research, and the men are 3x'ing it, creating a grandiose image that is romanticized by the investor, and ultimately invested in.

Chaya Cooper, a tech founder in New York City, shared her belief with me that when an investor is listening to a pitch, they should account for women's tendency to over-prepare, under promote, and undersell themselves, and being far more likely to err on the side of caution when pitching potential investors, partners or team members.

We have to make the knowledge of this overinflation by males and understatement by females more prevalent. Otherwise, we run the risk of having women believe that they come up with smaller ideas, or their ideas aren't at the same level as those of our male counterparts because we are more likely to be honest about our progress rather than overconfidently over-projecting.

Founders can do whatever they need to do to project an image about their company. I thoroughly believe that what we put out, we get back, and always putting our company and our work into its best light is a wonderful idea as long as that best light is truthful. It's hard to compete with people who over-project, whatever their reasons may be and whatever gender they may be.

But, I've noticed that the companies that really make it, and invoke real change, and are led by founders who speak truths and wisdom that can influence the next generation. This is because the company is rooted in projecting fairly, doing what it does best, and not creating too grandiose of an image so that they may never live up to it. Or, the press drummed up about and around their product is legitimate, and has been incurred organically, because their technology and innovation truly is newsworthy.

THAT type of idea is brewing inside of you, ready to find new life, gain publicity and influence entirely because of its own merit.

So, whether you're about to come up with your big idea or you already have it, remember to focus on the impact of the idea. It's all too easy to get caught up in the game of comparison. Another entrepreneur is always going to be doing a better or a bigger job landing the press attention or drumming up financial evaluations. But, it's about the *idea,* not how it's externally perceived.

To gauge how big your idea is in veracious terms, answer these questions:

1. Who is your customer base?
2. What problem does your customer have that you are solving—and how bad of a problem is it, really?
3. Similar to #2, what is the pain you are relieving for your customer, or the need you are meeting?

Once you've identified the impact that your idea can and will make, boo ya! You have an idea that no one, not even the Shark Tank winners or front-page features on *Forbes* magazine can touch. Every idea serves a beautiful purpose in this world. If it relieves the pain of your customer base, that's a truly big idea.

Remember that the world's response to our ideas and our companies are going to be very different than it is to the ideas and companies of others we know. It's hard to measure how "BIG" or successful an online publication will be, for example, in the context of virtual reality glasses. It isn't a competition.

As hard as we will all "hustle" for our BIG ideas, there's one beautiful quote I found that should remind you on the days you want to compare that all is happening as it should:

New York is three hours ahead of California, but that doesn't make California slow.

Someone graduated at the age of twenty-two, but waited five years before securing a good job.

Someone became a CEO at twenty-five, but died at fifty. While another became a CEO at fifty, and lived to ninety years.

Everyone in this world works based on their time zone. People around you might seem ahead of you, and some might seem behind you. But everyone is running their own race, in their own time.

There is no need to envy or mock anyone. They are in their own time zone and you are in yours. Life is about waiting for the right moment to act.

So relax. You're not late. You're not early.

You are very much on time.

~(AUTHOR UNKNOWN)

CHAPTER 3

THE FUTURE IS FEMALE

When I dare to be powerful, to use my strength in the service of my vision, then it becomes less and less important whether I am afraid.

~ AUDRE LORDE

I once asked Adrian France, one of my dear friends and the cofounder of wildly successful publication *The Odyssey*— "What's your best advice for female entrepreneurs?"

She replied: "Don't think of yourself as a female entrepreneur."

It wasn't the answer I was expecting! I was trying to differentiate a woman who pursues entrepreneurship from a man who pursues entrepreneurship in the question, but she posed an interesting consideration. It's just the same as saying, *"female* doctor,"" or *"girl* boss,"" instead of "doctor" or "boss." The image of a man comes to our heads. We're socialized to think that way, so we feel we have to specify.

But, that also makes it a marked difference because we all know we don't say "male entrepreneur."

To fully understand what it means to be a self-identifying woman pursuing entrepreneurship, we have to be aware of some of the stereotypes and misunderstandings surrounding WHO is an entrepreneur because they are reinforced at networking events, in venture capital firms, and anywhere that entrepreneurship is prevalent.

That is why this book is titled *Her BIG Idea*—not just *Your Big Idea*. It's gender-specific because to make change, we have to have honest conversations about where the entrepreneurial sphere is falling short for women.

DOES AN ENTREPRENEUR HAVE TO BE MALE?

Well, no. But it sure seems like it.

When you're reading through articles or essays on entrepreneurship, the "he" is used interchangeably with entrepreneur.

People like me pick up on this—perks of having studied Gender Studies in college.

But it's so subtle and so ingrained that we seldom pick it up when it occurs. I wanted to dig further into why exactly this is. Yes, it's true that women only own 5 percent of all startups. And, it's true that since the days of the first railroad, we've imagined a MAN as the head of the show, running the business, the top executive.

But, there's something inherent in *entrepreneurship* particularly that seems to be a masculine trait. Entrepreneurs have to go out there and GET it. They are bossy. They have a vision they don't waiver from. They send hundreds of emails, make hundreds of calls. They're in your face. They work long hours.

They know what they want, and they go out to get it.

Thinking way back to historical times, an archetype emerged about men and imperialism. They would stake their nation's flag into the soil of new land, claiming the territory and the people within it as theirs. Men would argue and summon wars costing hundreds of thousands of lives over territory and power. This sense of ownership and needing to claim what one wants is, well, a bit like entrepreneurship.

You want a customer segment. You want your target market. And a few things are necessary to make that happen. You NEED a meeting with that key connection. You NEED publicity in this or that magazine. Your life very quickly becomes about the chase—pouncing on opportunity and making new ones.

The stereotype of the entrepreneur is also the identity of a lone wolf. It's someone who often has to put feelings and emotions on the back burner. The time required to start a company also requires sacrifice—sacrifice of friends, time with family, time to work out, alone time. And, this ease in sacrificing is seen as "male," too, especially when it comes to family and relationships. We saw the shows in the 1950s about the idea of the nuclear family. The man was always apologizing for being late because of a busy day at the office and just wanted time to smoke his cigar at the day's end rather than spending time with his kids.

We know this idea of the male is so far removed from what's true and realistic, but stereotypes persist.

Our pal Sophia Amoruso had Netflix make her book, #Girlboss, and the story about her rise to success as a Netflix series that aired for a total of one season. This idea of the stubborn and reckless entrepreneur plays out in the bad taste of the character of Sophia in the show.

Those who reviewed it knew it. In a *Vanity Fair* article titled "In Netflix's *Girlboss*, The Emperor Has No Clothes," author Hillary Busis remarks about Sophia's character: "She's loud; she's brash; she's obnoxiously overconfident. She's a bad girlfriend and a worse friend-friend. She steals things, frequently and flagrantly—including, over the course of *Girlboss*'s first thirteen episodes, a rug, a copy of *Starting an eBay Business for Dummies* (twice), a bottle of Champagne, a stuffed monkey, a classic joke from *The Simpsons*, and a Christmas tree."[14]

But, this isn't just about one poorly executed show on Netflix. Rather, it's about how our previous conceptions of what an entrepreneur needs to be—the lone wolf type, prone to risk taking—hinders our ability to see the woman as entrepreneur. When the woman is put into the role of the entrepreneur in popular culture, she's seen as reckless and cutthroat. She's acting as the imperialist male figure would—taking things, destroying relationships, and being someone "who never says sorry."

But this is actually so far removed from reality and not how we really get things done. And, frankly, it's not how a lot of men get things done, either.

These conceptions are rapidly changing. But if we can identify how and why entrepreneurship and the roots of masculinity are so deeply associated, we can laugh at the crazy changes of time and turn our focus onto the women who made things happen and began the process of redefining who an entrepreneur is.

SILICON VALLEY & THE TECH BOOM

Another area that needs work for female empowerment is the tech space. Surprise!

Silicon Valley in particular is hailed as the "venture capital" capital of the world—where the best ideas are bolstered by the deep pockets of large and prestigious venture capital firms. It also has one defining characteristic that hails its monstrous success since the dot-com boom. It's solely for the tech elite and the greatest technical ideas.

The Facebooks, Tinders, Snapchats, and Ubers of the world that rise from this valley are started by predominately **white males** in hoodies and jeans.

In fact, a 2014 report by Fenwick & West LLP found that women only hold 11.8 percent of the executive positions in Silicon Valley.[15]

And faster than ever, these tech conglomerates have taken on a viral effect—growing, blazing and becoming what I call the BIG ideas—big enough to encompass billions of users, worldwide.

The rise of tech has raised the precedent for what a BIG idea really is because it's changed our conceptions of just how many people can use a product or service. Think about it. Roughly 158 million people use Snapchat every day, and those users open Snapchat about eighteen times a day. You can't say the same about the daily consumption of Barq's Root Beer, for instance.

The discrepancy between men and women creating these big tech ideas widens because of the small number of women in tech.

The discrepancy between the number of men and women pursuing an interest in tech begins to widen in elementary school and extends upward.

"The Interference of Stereotype Threat with Women's Generation of Mathematical Problem-Solving Strategies" by Diane Quinn and Steven Spencer states that "The belief that men are inherently better than women at math because they innately possess better mathematics aptitude and ability is widely and strongly held" and creates an attitude that limits performance potential in elementary school through high school, thus discouraging a woman's likelihood to choose a STEM major in college.[16]

Often, this is because the belief that "girls are bad at math" is pervasive in subtle ways. No one outright says it, but no one doesn't say it, either.

I once read an article in *TIME* magazine about a girl in an AP Computer Science course who aced her midterm—only for the teacher to accuse her of cheating.

But a girl gets a bad grade on her math test, she assumes she's bad at math, and no one really corrects that statement. But when a boy gets a bad grade on his math test, it's everyone's fault but his own—likely the teacher's. He brushes it off and likely rebounds, forgetting the bad test ever happened.

The girls that ARE good at math and enjoy it are particularly rare because that is discouraged on a peer-to-peer level; it isn't "cool" to be good at math, especially in the highly impressionable years of elementary school through middle school.

Unfortunately, these years are also highly influential for the long term of a woman's self-concept in her education and career. A friend of mine told me that her daughter, who was a fifth grader at the time, liked math but refused to join the math club because "girls aren't supposed to be good at math."

When girls get left behind in school, it creates a domino effect. Not only are women discouraged in school from pursuing degrees in the STEM field because of implicit biases, but as they get older, they have a lack of women in their network with strong technical backgrounds.

"Gender and Venture Capital Decision Making" by Justine E. Tinkler supports these assertions, stating: "the scarcity of women entrepreneurs reflects the shortage of women with education and experience in science and technology, or the absence of women in strategic entrepreneurial networks."[17]

This has repercussions far beyond the industry of one's knowledge, as Tinkler goes on: "In the context of venture capital, and considering the significance of technical credentials, not having a technical background may. . .confirm a woman entrepreneur's lack-of-fit with entrepreneurship, while having a technical background may be a strong indicator of performance ability and in turn, limit (and even reverse) perceived lack-of-fit."

This said, so many outstanding tech entrepreneurs are women. These women are pushing past the structural barriers that diminish their belief in their own capacity for tech. And, these women are coming up with BIG ideas.

Anne Wojcicki and Linda Avey are the founders of 23AndMe, the bio-tech testing and analysis survey in which you can order a kit, take a sample of your saliva, and send it off to a lab to receive in just six to eight weeks a detailed account of your ancestry and health.

Robin Chase is the founder of Zipcar, which is revolutionizing the transportation industry. Zipcar is a shared car service. Simply download the app, find a Zipcar near you, and get in for a spin. These vehicles even come with a gas card and track your usage by mileage and time spent in the car.

Jessica Livingston is the Founding Partner of Y Combinator, which is arguably the most prestigious startup accelerator of today, is thought to primarily fund tech startups. Y Combinator has funded some of the most powerful tech startups—Airbnb, Stripe, Reddit, Dropbox, Weebly...and the list goes on.

GIVE ME THAT MOOLA!

Last year (2017), only 2 percent of venture capital money went to companies founded by a female.[18]

Yep, you read that right.

This is probably the most horrifying statistic I have ever heard in my young life and is central to the theory of the BIG idea. Just as I define a BIG idea as one capable of generating millions and billions in revenue, it's obvious that cash is king in any business, and it's nearly impossible to get to those BIG numbers without a large upfront investment. You can't invest the money to build and develop an app, for example, if you're a young woman in college without any help from investors. And, you can't hire a team or spend a sizable budget on marketing without that extra cash.

A conversation with my friend Allie Felix, who previously worked for Draper University offered a suggestion: that the disproportionate number of men in the venture capital space created an environment where an understanding of products and services marketed to women was suppressed.

Allie shared that she watched a pitch at SoGal Ventures in which a female entrepreneur pitched a new and improved breast pump and needed the funding to expand her distribution channels. Tim Draper agreed to invest on the spot—he identified with her pain point because his daughter had just had a baby. But in other situations like this one, male venture capitalists would typically be scratching their heads at the numbers, unable to understand why exactly women needed this new breast pump. Unless they could empathize with the pain point, they wouldn't find the product worth investing in, because there is already a diverse selection of breast pumps on the market.

The investor *needs* to empathize with the pain point or problem to find a pith compelling.

It appears that a potential reason that female-founded companies receive less capital than male-founded companies is that the creator of a product is likely to create a product that fulfills their own unmet need. Think about it: Sara Blakely created Spanx unknowingly because she cut the feet portion out of her pantyhose. She solved her own problem and met her own (originally) unmet need. And it happened to be gendered, because whichever way you cut the pie, women wear pantyhose more often than men do.

A male venture capitalist would have scratched his head looking at the new contraption that used to be pantyhose. "*Why,*" he thinks, "*would women not need the feet?*"

I'm not making this up. Blakely herself laughs as she recalls trying to tell the male attorneys about how to make "women's butts better" and concomitantly "change the world." There wasn't exactly an enthusiastic response. In fact, she noticed one attorney continuously looking around the room rather than paying attention to her. He later told her that he thought her idea was so stupid at the time that he thought they were being pranked by Candid Camera.

So gender, as it pertains in the Spanx scenario, and really where discrepancies stand in Silicon Valley and beyond today poses an interesting question. Does the gender of the founder need to match the gender of the product's market?

Dan Aziz is a Brown graduate who created a prenatal vitamin supplement during an entrepreneurship course in undergrad (a course that changed my very life, which we will get to). But the idea itself didn't strike him in its current form. He actually went out looking for it.

His group knew they wanted to do something in the health sector, and where better to look for hints of problems than Whole Foods? After perusing the aisles of a Whole Foods in Providence and conducting some of this good ol' market research, he noticed pregnant women in the vitamin aisle, appearing noticeably distressed as they read the descriptions of the prenatal vitamin bottles. So, he approached them and started to ask some questions, trying to get to the bottom of why this was causing such discomfort and dissatisfaction.

Turns out that prenatal vitamins are quite a pill (pun intended) to swallow. They're big, obnoxious to lug around, and can amplify morning sickness.

So, he created a prenatal supplement called Premama that works in much of the same way a packet of Emergen-C or Crystal Lite does. It's flavored and turns a bottle of water into a tasty, healthy delight rather than a chaser for a pill the size of Texas. It's seen extraordinary success that is only growing to a greater magnitude as it spreads to new distributors and increases its product line, including a supplement for breast-feeding mothers.

Although founders who are meeting their unmet need with their product are constant self-reminders about the market for their product, BIG ideas often lie somewhere out there, in uncharted territory. Being aware of others' inconveniences with an objectivity can also spark ideas for innovation that will change just as many lives, or at least make them a bit easier. Yes, YOU, can create a product exclusively for men that will be successful! It's not only a man's realm out there.

I asked Dan what it was like to pitch Premama to male investors, as investors hope to see that the team they may invest in has an unfair competitive advantage in the industry or with the ability to make the product. He was honest with me: "There was a lot of wondering from the investors, 'why you?' Why was I equipped to make this product? I'm a male in my mid-twenties. I know nothing about pregnancy or prenatal supplements." This lit a fire in him to drive home the pitch and to make the numbers from his market research and initial sales count.

"I've seen incredible pitches by women and lackluster pitches from men," he told me. "It's really a matter of how well they've done their market research. It comes down to the idea. Is it a good idea? Have they proved it can sell?"

Regardless of who you are and your personal need for your product (or lack thereof), there are pitches that blow the roof off the barn with praise and wows, and there are those that flop. Harness the power of market research for your product. Numbers don't lie, and it's a compelling way to make someone listen if they don't have a personal affirmation with your idea. Just as I previously mentioned that I am not an exercise program aficionado—you bet your bottom dollar that if I was an investor, and the exercise program creator strolled in and pitched their idea with such gusto, research, and skyrocketing numbers, I'd be shoveling over the money faster than I could sprint.

A presentation called "VC Decision-Making, Networks, and Geographies" presented by Professor Banu Özkazanç-Pan and Professor Paolo Gaudiano shared that all-female firms often invest small seed amounts (think $10,000) rather than the *big* money amounts ($5 million and upward) that we see invested from predominantly male firms in Silicon Valley.[19] Their research finds that 12% of venture rounds and 10% of venture dollars globally between 2010 and 2015 wen to startups with at least one-woman founder, whereas 17% of seed rounds and 15% of seed dollars globally between the same time period went to startups with at least one woman founder.

Thus, venture capital would be much more equitable if there were an equal number of men and women at each venture capital firm rather than an equal number of all male and all female venture capital firms. Professors Özkazanç-Pan and Gaudiano also stated something that was incredibly useful for our conceptualization: venture capital only funds about 2 percent of all companies. But, venture capital occupies such a large part of our social imaginary, and we give it so much importance, that we need to ensure it is promoting equality.

The other side of the realization that venture capital *does* occupy such importance in our social imaginary despite its relatively minuscule influence should remind us that our perception of the world is seldom rooted in truth. Reality is subjective. The greatest entrepreneurs can mold situations to their advantage, as the Effectuation Theory explains. They do not wait to see how it turns out and feel doomed to external circumstances. They create their own circumstances.

SO, WHAT NOW?

I'll admit it—this chapter was a bit grim. It's hard to read statistics like these and be hopeful, given all this evidence that we are in the minority.

But I truly believe acknowledging structural inequalities and long-stated biases about female capacity is what we need to do to move into the age of the female. Nothing ever gets moved, shaken, or shattered by being ignored.

We can call out these biases by pushing back—by celebrating more female entrepreneurs and rallying the power. We are in an age of social progress. So much has changed just in the past fifty years—imagine the next fifty!—especially at the rate in which women are trying out entrepreneurship. The American Express "2016 State of Women-Owned Businesses Report" found that "the number of women-owned firms has grown at a rate fully five times faster than the national average."[20]

We are at the greatest hindrance when we are hyperaware that we could be at a disadvantage in certain spaces—the networking events with mostly men and the venture capital firms. So, what if we seek to disprove our limitations?

An entrepreneur goes out there and gets it done. They hustle. They burn the midnight oil. They call someone's assistant fifty times a day and send bouquets of flowers for a meeting. They know what they want and they go after that vision. So many of us female founders go through these motions but feel an inherent sense of dis-ease, believing that we won't be taken as seriously as a man—which is a valid concern. But this fear can and will be shattered the more we prove to ourselves that gender should not be an asterisk or even a consideration.

We are *entrepreneurs* if we create something beyond ourselves. We are *entrepreneurs* if we are putting something into the world that heightens efficiency and solves problems. And gender has very little—if not nothing—to do with that at all.

So, what are you? AN ENTREPRENEUR.

And the future for entrepreneurs is female.

CHAPTER 4

START TO THINK BIG

---

*When you believe something is impossible, your mind goes
to work for you to prove why. But when you believe, really
believe, something can be done, your mind goes to work for
you and helps you find the ways to do it.*

~ DAVID J. SCHWARTZ, *THE MAGIC OF THINKING BIG* [21]

When we were children, we'd play make-believe with some
pretty radical storylines.

Some of us believed in Santa Claus, the Easter Bunny, the
Tooth Fairy. We seriously were able to comprehend that these
fictional and adorable characters could circle the world in one
night and leave treats for all the children.

Thinking this big was encouraged! We were told that something out there was really that nonsensical, but it made sense to us because adults had to know what they were talking about. (Also likely: We weren't in a rush to put up a fight about presents on an annual basis.) So, we penned our hopeful letters to Santa, put our hard-won lost baby teeth under our pillows, and didn't stop to ask questions about the sense of it all.

We got to a point, eventually, where we had to put a constraint on how big we could think or conceptualize. Despite how some of our parents encouraged us to think big during our childhoods, we witnessed societal standards of restraint, urging us to mitigate risk. This pressured us to tone down our big dreams for the realistic ones, if for nothing less than to fit in with the other small-minded thinkers. Small thinking was simply safer.

We've carried this doomed sense of reality with us ever since. It's the same inner voice that tells us to expect the worse and buy insurance. It's the same inner voice that encourages us to call dreams of becoming famous singers or winning a Nobel Prize "pipe dreams." These adventures and achievements seem so *big* that they seem impossible. We are unintentionally socialized to think small about our lives and our capacities for greatness. With all that small thinking going on, it's no wonder that the big ideas are so hard to come by.

But sometimes, if we get silent with ourselves, we can tap into something that's begging to be bigger. I'm especially talking to you here because there's a reason you picked up this book. There's a reason you wanted to think big or do something big—and you can, and you will.

So, why do you think it is that you don't think big enough on your own?

Maybe, you're scared.

It's scary to get outside your comfort zone and think about something that has never been done before. What if you totally fall in love with the big idea? Doesn't that mean you have to do it and bring it into this world? And oh, no, I am NOT equipped for that.

The most life-changing course I've taken was my first business course at Brown: The Entrepreneurial Process with Professor Danny Warshay. Danny is the Executive Director of Brown's Nelson Center for Entrepreneurship and has inspired me with his big thinking from day one in his classroom. After graduating from Brown, he co-founded a company that was sold to Apple and went on to receive his MBA from Harvard

Business School. Today, in addition to his professorship at Brown, he teaches his entrepreneurial process in workshops around the world, from Yale to Tel Aviv, and with organizations like Seeds of Peace in Jordan. A bedrock principle of his entrepreneurial process is thinking big.

In fact, if it wasn't for him, this book would probably be called "Her Idea."

He dispels the persistent myth that big thinking is crazy thinking. He shares the truth that big thinking is actually the best way to counteract risk; if you half-bake this entrepreneurship thing, it isn't going to be a good enough cookie. Thinking small and going after small ideas seems safe, but you're actually more likely to fail if you do so.

One of the greatest all-time venture capitalists, Arthur Rock, invested in big-name companies like Apple and Intel, and he stated that his sole criteria for seeking investment opportunities is this: "Look for business concepts that will change the way people *live* or *work*." [22]

If you're going to put your whole, one life into your big idea, it better be an idea that changes the game, and quadruples your annual salary.

This has a direct impact on the likelihood of success. The same book that shares Arthur Rock's wisdom notes the threshold is called *New Venture Creation: Entrepreneurship for the 21st Century*. It goes on about big ideas: "The odds for survival and a higher level of success change dramatically if the venture reaches a critical mass of at least ten to twenty million people with $2–3 million in revenues and is currently pursuing opportunities with growth potential."

Oh, the big get bigger.

Many years ago, when Oprah Winfrey was just a girl, she was doing laundry with her grandmother in Mississippi and her grandmother told her to "Watch closely because you'll be doing this for a long, long time." Oprah recalls that she didn't believe it because she didn't feel it. She knew deep in her being that she was bigger than laundry, bigger than Mississippi, and "bigger than what Mississippi thought of her." I'm willing to bet that you've had moments with this same glimmer of intuition.

To get to what's big, we have to give ourselves permission to dream again. We know the vision we have for our life—and now it's time to amplify it. Striving for a future that seems "great" and has "what you want" is sufficient, but we can't think big unless we strive for a future that obliterates expectations and makes your heart race. Unless we think about a vision for our lives that changes the way we live and work—similar to Arthur Rock's criteria.

Similar to the truth that we haven't been taught to forge a new industry with our idea, we haven't been taught to feel we have momentous control over our circumstances. When you've envisioned yourself driving that Rolls Royce or spending the rest of your days gallivanting on the white sands of Fiji, you've had a million different "insurance" voices telling you why that can't be. "What the heck am I going to do that will sustain me in that mansion in Fiji?" Self-Doubt Sally whines.

Well, it's just that, you can't rationalize the big. You can only put it out there and then trust that the path to it will become visible as you go. We can't start by making the plan. We can only start with our vision of the destination.

Anything's possible if you have enough nerve.

~J.K. ROWLING

The best way to do this, in my experience, is to make a vision board.

Some of you may scoff at this, thinking it's some voodoo Law of Attraction practice, but humor me. Worst case scenario, you have a fun and creative afternoon with arts and crafts.

Sit down with some magazines, your computer, a printer, some scissors, tape, and pens—and start to look for what you want in your life. Play some pump-up music. You'll be surprised what pops out at you as you thumb through magazines—words like "refreshed" and phrases like "all that glitters is gold" will transform from marketing lines to words to describe your best life, alongside photos of experiences or material objects that evoke a feeling of desire.

I make a vision board every New Year's Day of what I want for the year, which is a great way to do it because my visions have become grander as the years have gone on and I've become more comfortable with desiring more. The evolution of your vision for your life is inevitable, and we want it to expand. And, yes, each of them have come true for me, personally—from the golden doodle to my first time peering at the Eiffel Tower.

These visions come to fruition because of the incredible power of our brain's neuro-elasticity. *Psychology Today* reported that, when watching weight-lifters lift heavy weights, the same neural pathways light up in the spectator's brain that light up when the spectator is lifting heavy weights themselves. They're called *mirror neurons.*[23]

So, our brain experiences what we envision, regardless of if our body is actually experiencing it. This is how Olympic athletes visualize performance, so they may perform in atonement with their optimal visualizations. All that can happen in that noggin of yours.

Take it from a few celebrities:

Jim Carey wrote himself a check for $10 million for acting services rendered, dated it for the date he hoped to achieve it, and signed for *Dumb and Dumber* for $10 million right before that date.

In fourth grade, Katy Perry made a vision board with a picture of Selena accepting a Grammy—envisioning herself as the next Selena. She won her first Grammy fifteen years later.

Beyoncé had a picture of an Academy Award in front of her treadmill, so she could look at it daily while she ran. The movie she starred in, *Dream Girls*, won an Academy Award.

Our friend Sara Blakeley, founder of Spanx, didn't even make a vision board. She just wrote down her goals. She simply focused on the goals: "To be self-employed, to make a product that will sell to many, and a company that will fund itself."

You may be thinking, Well, that's just sheer luck. Or, they're so talented! When am I going to be able to sing like Beyoncé? But, we all have marketable talents inside of us.

One of my favorite all-time quotes is by Sonia Sotomayor in her book, *My Beloved World:*

> But experience has taught me that you cannot value dreams according to the odds of their coming true. Their real value is in stirring within us the will to aspire. That will, wherever it finally leads, does at least move you forward.[24]

Doug Bate is an innovation consultant, life coach, and one of the most influential mentors in my life. I attended a session he hosted at Brown called "Create Your Life." He believes firmly in the power of vision boards to get real on what our soul really wants to do.

He stressed the dissonance that occurs when we conjure a big dream for ourselves and then see where we are now. It seems like a huge jump. We can't logically imagine what the heck we're going to do to get from Point A to Point B. It seems outside our control, like getting discovered, or winning the lottery. But, he urges that opening ourselves to BIG thinking about the grandest vision we can have for our life opens our eyes to opportunities beyond what we can currently see. When we're clear on what we WANT, our brain is wired to recognize opportunities that we were closed off to before.

Our brains are like computers. They receive about 34GB of information a day, flying at warp speed, while we're worried about whether we turned off our hair curler or what the traffic will be like later.

To break this down even further, we're bombarded with six hundred billion bits of information every second. And yet, we're only able to process about twenty-five hundred bits per second. Our poor brains get overwhelmed and have to process only what seems important. Things that require immediate attention—face-to-face conversations, deadlines, to-do lists—are the first to be processed. Which means we're literally walking around with blinders on, completely oblivious to opportunities that are smack in front of our faces.

We are blind to, well, 599,999,997,500 bits of information every second that could potentially be important, or a hint toward our dreams, or a glimpse of an opportunity.

Imagine that an accountant has a dream to start her own restaurant. She's frustrated because she has to crunch numbers all day in a cubicle and has no time to start a business plan, facilitate connections, or get a start on any progress toward this dream. So, she puts it to the side and calls it a "pipe dream."

But then, when she's pouring creamer in her coffee at the coffee shop on Monday morning, she isn't aware of opportunities in front of her—the flyer smack in front of her face about a new five-star restaurant hiring a head chef to start immediately. Even just looking out the window briefly and allowing her eyes to graze past the word "chef" or "restaurant" can *ding ding* in the brain if she's fixated on the goal. This one registration can lead to a chain of events that reveals the path from A to B in front of her. She gets the job as head chef, takes creative liberties with the menu, and the owner of the restaurant asks her to take over when she retires.

I know this seems like a wild chain of events, but one of my favorite quotes of all time by Steve Jobs alludes to just this: *"You cannot connect the dots looking forward, you can only connect the dots looking back."*

Everything in your life has been a series of serendipitous happenings. Reveling in that will send shivers down your spine. If you doubt that for a second, reflect on one instance in your life recently that seemed "lucky" or "out of the blue," and think of everything that had to happen to lead to that moment. The people you had to meet, conversations you had to have. You created its appearance in your reality.

So, open yourself up to a new chain of serendipitous events. You get to choose which events and which opportunities unfold. I hope that's empowering to you.

But, before you take out the planner, ready to plan your chain of serendipitous events, know this:

Doug told me that when we make plans, we'll never get to where we're heading.

1. A plan will never excite you as much as jumping in will, so the plan will never spur to action.

2. Creating a plan confers an element of risk in our brains, so we can scare ourselves out of going for it before we even begin.

3. Plans are made to be broken. How the heck are you supposed to know which array of circumstances will compel the next step?

So, the only thing to do is ditch the plan and *jump in*.

Put your vision board somewhere you'll see it every day—right above your desk, across from your bed, or in front of your treadmill like Beyoncé did. Remember, your vision board is supposed to conjure a strong positive emotion, something that will motivate you on the days you're lacking motivation. Trust that your emotions and your brain alone can make you buzz on a higher frequency, more able to see opportunities as they unfold. The path there always reveals itself. *It's not your job to have the answers.* It's your job do the best you can and to believe that it will get you where you want to go.

Our lives are comprised of many small days where we do our best, say prayers, make wishes, work hard, and dream big.

Pursuing a big idea is much of the same. But when you're chipping away at the small tasks to make your big idea come to life, keep that vision alive. You don't have to do the big to get the big, nor should you. It's impossible. Do all you can in the time you're allotted, and in time, it will become the big.

TALKING CANDY

I first met Doug Bate in Danny Warshay's class; he came to talk to us about his business experience. This was during the phase of class where we were first starting to put together business plans and think of ideas to develop in groups. At this time, I didn't realize that big thinking played any role in the creation of a company. In my head, a group of executives would sit around a round table, pots of black coffee coursing through their veins, and spitball totally rational ideas that everyone could understand. It's how all of my ideas had come to me, but admittedly, I was your typical sufferer of the Small Idea Syndrome and wasn't thinking up the next Apple (yet).

While vision boards can get us thinking in our optimal big state for what we want for our personal lives, a bit more goes into it when we begin to think of a business idea.

The thing about big business ideas is that they take that extra push—that excruciating stretch beyond your comfort zone, like when you were learning how to do the splits as a kid. It's supposed to boggle your brain—something that we can hardly envision because it's so far off reality. It reminds me of when I handed my grandfather one of the first iPhones, and he stared in wonder at the screen, completely amazed that it responded to his finger touch and could even tell you the weather!

What is that product that your grandchildren and great-grandchildren will introduce to you that will leave you totally amazed? In order to come up with a truly and terrifically BIG idea, it has to be something that no one has thought of in its entirety before. There are exercises out there that help you get there, and the rule of the game is to think of something as Nonsensical, Outrageous, and Wacky as possible, condense it to realistic proportions, and create it.

This brings me to the story of all stories in the BIG idea creation process: the creation of Talking Candy. You know a talking candy, and you don't even know it yet. You may have even tried it. But before it was a real product it was a nonsensical, outrageous, and wacky idea that struck the right group of people at the right time.

Rumor has it that a group got together at General Foods a number of years ago and needed to think big. So, they start spit balling, thinking of the Next Best Product for General Foods. They're using things they know, trying to re-imagine chocolate, hoping for a breakthrough to strike. Then, someone says, "Gee, I wish there was a way to get candy to talk."

Next thing you know, someone else in the group knows a chemist named William A. Mitchell who just accidentally created a substance that could imitate a "chit chat" upon contact with saliva, and, well, that's how Pop Rocks were created.

Doug Bate attributes this crazy strike of genius to an "invisible component" that is subtly beneath the surface of any creation. Innovation is really putting two things together that have never before been paired. It was the first time that candy wasn't just about taste. It was suddenly about sound and sensation.

You can't make a big idea with something that already exists. You can, however, take TWO things that already exist and seem totally incompatible—talking and candy, *per esempio*—and make something bigger than the two.

The wildest ideas bring the magic of the latest scientific discoveries or hidden talents to life. The power we have in imagination and make-believe is what gives life to ordinary objects or basic chemistry.

CHAPTER 5

HERE COMES THE *BIG*

———

An idea that is not dangerous is unworthy of being called an idea at all.

~ OSCAR WILDE

J. K. Rowling had the idea for Harry Potter when she was on a train, but she didn't have a pen with her.

The idea for a multimillion-dollar book series (unbeknownst to her, of course, at the time) had just fallen into her head, and the poor thing didn't even have a pen to write it all down!

We all know that eventually, she found a pen, and this one awe-inspiring moment led to a $15 billion brand. How lucky is that? Or is it?

IDEAS VIA STORKS

Where do ideas come from? The Harry Potter one seemed
to fall from the sky upon unsuspecting and unprepared J. K.
Rowling. It usurped her. That idea was its own entity, and it
decided it was time to be born and go out into the world and
entertain the population, so that's just what it did.

If you ask other entrepreneurs or creators how their ideas
came, a good majority of people are going to say, "It came
to me when I was in the shower," or, "It came to me when I
was driving."

It's true that during these mindless, mundane everyday tasks,
we enter a mental state where things flow and connect effort-
lessly, and the fruits of our experiences and insights click like
a Rubik's Cube. Scientists have studied this phenomenon and
believe it can be partially due to the release of dopamine in
our brains, which sparks creativity. When we enter a relaxed
state—such as when we're showering or driving—creativity
is easier to access.

Jonah Lehrer, an author who studied neuroscience at Columbia University, explains it this way in his book *Imagine: How Creativity Works*:

> When our minds are at ease—when those alpha waves are rippling through the brain—we're more likely to direct the spotlight of attention inward, toward that stream of remote associations emanating from the right hemisphere.[25]

In other words, ideas click together when we're in our own heads without any distractions. Those alpha waves only flow through our brains when we're in a relaxed state, and this is when ideas knock on the front door and ask to come in. They're unexpected, but always welcome. And, they seem to create themselves. They come from bits and pieces of research we have read and what we have observed. They click together just so. It's an "epiphany."

As NPR quotes from an "All Things Considered" segment on Lehrer's book: "The brain is just an endless knot of connections. And a creative thought is simply . . . a network that's connecting itself in a new way."[26]

You can't, unfortunately, sit down at your desk in front of a blank sheet of paper and command ideas to come. The greatest creations and innovations come in much of the same way the flow of writing comes. It wells from deeper within us, arises with euphoria, and takes on an otherworldly form. You likely know the feeling from one or two of your creations. You're left wondering, "Did that really come from me?"

I like to think that it's not always something that came from us and our brains—but something we received, like a gift from the other side. This is similar to how I feel when I write. I believe we can become vessels for something greater to move through us, if only we have the confidence to bring it to life.

My favorite, favorite book is *Big Magic* by Elizabeth Gilbert. If you're a writer or at all a creative person, I urge you to go onto Amazon and order it at the end of this chapter. And once you begin, you'll read this story.

After her hit novel *Eat, Pray, Love* was published, Gilbert's now-husband told her a story that completely boggled her— that, many, many years ago, a number of big shot investors invested millions of dollars into constructing a highway through the Amazon rainforest.

This was going to be quite the project and required a LOT of capital. But, they got to work, and the bolstering bulldozers came to the scene, and . . .

Monsoon season started.

It's striking how she explains the story, but I mean really guys, did we forget that the Amazon is subject to some wild rains during the calendar year?

It rained and rained and rained, until the soil melted to mud, and the ground swallowed up the bulldozers. This image, if you can picture it now, is pretty chilling. And, our pal Elizabeth Gilbert thought so too.

So, she came up with a book idea around this very happening. She created a plot line based on an unhappy woman named Evelyn who leaves her husband to go down to the Amazon and falls madly in love with a businessman she meets down there. She planned to title the book *Evelyn of the Amazon*. (Is Elizabeth amazing, or what?)

She got the green light from her publisher and started writing away. But then, personal life events came up, and Gilbert had to put the book on the back burner for a while until they were settled. When she finally came back to the book, it had lost its magic, its life. She couldn't revive it. She remembers feeling that it was all wrong.

Right around the same time, just a few weeks beforehand, she had been to a book signing of an author she greatly admired named Ann Patchett. She and Ann were elated to meet each other—so much so that Elizabeth actually kissed her cheek at the signing. They got to talking and developed a fabulous friendship—and, a few months later, met up for coffee to catch up.

Ann told her she had a new idea for a book. . . and lo and behold, it was about the Amazon construction project. She had already begun to write the book, which is now published and titled *State of Wonder*.

Right down to the last detail of falling in love with a businessman down at the Amazon while the ground swallowed bulldozers whole, Ann had the SAME IDEA as Elizabeth.

And Elizabeth knew she could think malevolently of this snafu. She could accuse her new friend of somehow finding out about her idea and taking it. But she was sure that this didn't happen at all; in fact, she believed that when they met, a kiss upon Ann's cheek "transferred" the idea. And that's really the stuff of magic.

It was her first powerful indication that ideas are collective. We must become quiet and let them come to us. It really is a radical notion—that somewhere out "there," wherever "there is," is this untapped realm of ideas. Unwritten songs and books, undiscovered cures, unpursued business ideas, and they're all ours for the taking if we allow them to come to us.

THE IDEA COLLECTIVE

Ideas don't always have to come to us when we're conscious.

I was always intrigued by Stephanie Meyer and the *Twilight* series. Meyer had a dream one night about a vampire and a girl, and it was so riveting and heartbreaking to her that she knew she had to write about it.

It's my personal belief that when we dream, we tap the Collective—not just of ideas, but of facts and knowledge. I've had some spooky encounters with this myself and believe that Deja Vu is really just something we've dreamt of vividly beforehand. Pay attention to your dreams, even if it's just a storyline. Pay attention to what sticks.

But, there's a sense of dis-ease here. The lingering problem with tapping into the Collective is that it means your idea is up for grabs, or that it's not actually *your* idea. If it's in the Collective, it's accessible to others. How many times have you thought of something just to discover someone else thought of it already? How many times have you tried to secure a domain name, only to realize someone else had already secured the

.com AND .org of a business name you thought was unique? Why do we need trademark and patent attorneys—down to even the names of companies and slogans? Somewhere, someone has the same idea that is in your head, right now.

It's up to you to pursue it first and douse it in the magic that's uniquely yours.

The "Idea Collective" does *not* deny the power of your own creative touch. You, after all, must name the characters, or articulate the value, or dream up the branding. But, it should be a call to action to get your ideas out of your head and make them into something before someone else does. Pay attention to ideas that really bug you—ones that would aggravate you if someone else were to pursue them. Trust that what seems to be a good idea to you is a good idea, period.

Eric Koester, my book coach and a Professor of Practice at the Georgetown University McDonough School of Business, told me as I compiled my research for this book—*to write what inspires me*. He discouraged me from first coming up with an outline and making the book I *should* write. Instead, if I write about what's inspired me personally, it will resonate and inspire you. If you pursue an idea that matters to you and has taken on a vibrant life within that beautiful brain of yours, it will resonate with others. Trust in this—and get that idea out there.

BUT, I'M AN IDEA MACHINE!

There is a small hiccup in this plan, of course, especially for people like me. I think of new business ideas constantly. They come to me in the typical places like the shower and the car, but also mid-conversation, or mid final exam—assuredly inconvenient times when I can't write them down. I urge you—try your best to make a list despite the inconvenience! Keep ideas in your head because they're fleeting. I will often have a waterfall of ideas in the shower and won't be able to remember half of them by the time I'm out of there, with my notebook. (Side note: If this happens to you, too, I was recommended a product while writing this book called "Aqua Notes." They're waterproof note pads so you can take notes right then and there in between suds.)

Once an idea comes to you, ride that wave all the way home, my friend. If you have the time allotted, write about it until the cows come home. I've found that in the "creative zone," more and more starts to flow, and the idea takes on a life that continues to grow and glow as I ruminate upon it.

THE MAD HATTER

I have deep respect and admiration for a certain type of person who has big ideas.

One of the following two conditions could be true about them:

1. *They're actually onto something world-changing and they're going to pioneer the future of humanity or*
2. *They're completely wrong and a little crazy, but they have mustered the courage to be publicly outspoken.*

~ADAM HESCH

One day this past December over a casual happy hour, my friend Adam said the above quote. It wasn't something he had written down previously and he said it in passing, in the midst of a longer discussion about entrepreneurs he knows. When he said "big idea," however, my ears perked up, and after he said the above, I whipped out my phone to ask him to repeat what he just said so I could write it down and capture it.

It reminds me of a line from the song "Audition (Fools Who Dream)" from the hit movie *La La Land*: "A little madness is key, to bring out new colors to see." Sometimes, being unafraid to be absolutely mad or stupendous can bring us to the next BIG idea. We've been taught our entire lives to be sane and to act sane—to be creative but to constrain our creativity to the arts, and to be curious but constrain our curiosity to the sciences. We are seldom taught to "think outside the box" or stray from the "right" path. But so often, the ones of us who refuse to follow the status quo or exercise self-constraint make millions and impacts millions.

Here's a list that will surprise you and likely make you laugh, but remember that the founder has the last laugh because they pocketed millions from these "crazy," "mad" ideas. They're not all BIG in the way I like, but hey, they'll get you thinking, and get you putting on your creativity goggles.

1. **The Pet Rock**. Remember a few years back when you could literally buy yourself a pet rock? Never mind that you could find a perfectly decent rock in, you know, your own back-yard. You needed it to come with a manual, a carrier, and of course a hay bed. Well, the first six months of this creation yielded its founder over $15 million.

2. **Slap Bracelets**. Another flashback to childhood. Remember slapping the stick-like contraption on your wrist to have it coil and wrap around your wrist perfectly, like a bracelet? Hours of fun!

3. **Crazy Straws**. You know nothing could make your dreaded daily cup of milk more fun than a "crazy straw." Winding and whistling from the cup to your mouth, these pops of color became sustainably successful.

4. **Velcro**. I'm not going to discount how useful Velcro really is, but the founder, Swiss engineer George de Mestral, thought of the idea when he saw how burrs stuck to his pants while he was on a camping trip. It takes someone really in the "creative zone" to turn an annoyance like that into a million-dollar idea! [27]

5. **The Slinky**. Ah, we all had one—such joy as it careened down stairwells! The founder witnessed a spring do the "crawling" motion after it fell and thought it might make a delightful household toy. Let's be honest, most of us would've just been annoyed that we had to run down the stairs after the spring. [28]

This list extends on and on. In fact, I only chose the ones you might recognize intentionally. I chose to forego, for example the dog goggles story (which are exactly what they sound like and yes, also made millions). But the moral of the story here is that we all have access to ideas that can make millions. The ones of us who do something with the crazy and the mad can achieve it.

Once we start to think creatively, everything becomes an opportunity for a new product. It doesn't have to be the next Tesla. Think about coffee sleeves, paperclips, tape—seemingly ordinary objects that we use every day that were dreamt up in the head of someone who had a vision. And, they have the annual paychecks to prove it was worthwhile.

Then, there are the ideas that came about purely by accident. I just wish I could've been a fly on the wall for some of these. It takes a special type of person to turn an "uh-oh" moment into a "Eureka!" moment.

These have always intrigued me, ever since my dad told me in my childhood that the ice cream I was licking was perched atop an accidental invention—the ice cream cone. It was mind-boggling to my six-year-old self how anyone could invent ANYTHING accidentally, let alone something as magical and central to my life as an ice cream cone.

But, it's true. At the 1904 World Fair, the ice cream stand was running out of plates for its long line, and the waffle stand next door wasn't selling anything. So, a miracle of the minds occurred, and they rolled up the waffles to hold the ice cream, which is why the waffle cone is a favorite.[29]

1. **Chocolate Chip Cookies**. Chocolate chip cookies were created when a cookie shop received an order for chocolate cookies but was out of cocoa. The chef, Ruth Graves Wakefield, put chopped up chocolate into the cookie dough, expecting the chocolate to melt in the oven. To her surprise, they didn't, but she had just invented the most popular cookie of all time. She could have thought, upon taking the tray of cookies out of the oven, "What a disaster!" thrown them in the trash, and run to the nearest store to grab some cocoa. But she saw the potential for something new and different. It just happened to become a BIG idea. (An aside: Wakefield sold her idea to Nestle because the chocolate she used was Nestle. In exchange, they gave her a lifetime of free chocolate. Sounds like a good deal to me!)[30]

2. **Coca-Cola**. Yes, one of the greatest beverage conglomerates in the world was created by accident. Pharmacist John Pemberton was actually just trying to make a medicine and made the scrumptious, sugar-filled delight that we sip during movies and with our hamburgers. Also, the original recipe had cocaine in it, so that's a fun fact.[31]

3. **Popsicles.** These delights were accidentally made by an eleven-year-old. How many of us weren't allowed to have soda

as kids? (Me!) Well, Frank Epperson was allowed to, but he didn't want to spend the money on it. So, he had the amazing idea to make his own with some sugary soda powder and proceeded to forgetfully leave his creation on the porch overnight. In the morning, he discovered that frozen soda is just as good as normal soda, if not better. He then began to sell it at a nearby amusement park, and eventually applied for a patent.[32]

4. **Potato Chips**. Rumor has it that back in 1853, a customer dining at the Moon Lake Lodge Resort in Saratoga Springs, New York returned their French fries to the chef, saying they were too thick. The chef, George Crum, cut the potatoes into thinner slices to make thinner fries—and still, the customer was not pleased. In an attempt to annoy the bossy customer, Crum cut the potatoes as thinly as he could, resulting in the crispy goodness we now call potato chips. They were an instant hit, and used to be called "Saratoga Chips" in honor of their place of origin.[33]

5. **Corn Flakes**. Will Keith Kellogg (does that last name sound familiar?) was in charge of making the bread when he was helping his brother, a doctor, at a sanitarium. But, he must have been off his bread-making game on this fateful day because he accidentally left boiled wheat sitting out for a few hours. He shrugged it off and threw it into the dough but realized when rolling it that it became flaky. After being cooked, corn flakes were created, and he happened to have

the perfect audience for market research. The patients at the hospital loved it and, well, now we have cornflakes and countless other cereals.[34]

None of these accidents, as "lucky" as they seem, were really determined by luck. They're determined by perspective, and the ability to see a mistake differently. Will Keith Kellogg could've thrown out that batch of dough upon finding it was flaky. Frank Epperson could've put his popsicles out in the sun and waited for them to melt back into the soda he'd intended. We don't have to stumble across accidents because who knows how many times we HAVE accidentally created or discovered something but haven't noticed it?

The ability to see the POSSIBLE in the ORDINARY is a defining characteristic of an entrepreneur who comes up with a BIG idea. That ability can and will enable you to find your idea in your own way.

CHAPTER 6

OPPORTUNITIES ABOUND

Opportunities multiply as they are seized.

Rent the Runway is my favorite company of all time.

Cofounded by Harvard Business School MBAs Jenny Fleiss and Jennifer Hyman, the company rents expensive designer dresses (and bags, jackets, and other clothing items) at 10–15 percent the retail price to consumers who are looking for a lower price point. They explain their value proposition as "democratizing luxury." Allowing college-aged women on a ramen budget to wear Badgley Mischka gowns to their cousin's wedding converts the women into lifelong Badgley Mischka customers from this mystical experience. Once they can afford to own their own B.M. dress, they will.

Their business model necessitates the purchasing of designer-brand clothes so they can then rent them out to their customers. And, on their initial phone calls with designers to ask if they'd be willing to feature their dresses as a Rent the Runway offering, the general response was, to quote their Harvard Business School case: "Over my dead body."

I mean, think about it. If you were a designer that could sell your famous sweetheart neckline casual workday dress for $1,000+ a pop, why would you want this new startup making money off your dress, with consumers out of your market segment paying a tiny price to wear it once?

Jenny and Jennifer knew they had just a few chances to prove their name and their ability to bring new consumers to the designer brand, converting them to lifelong customers. They needed the help of a seasoned and well-respected designer in the industry to give them their push.

Diane von Furstenberg was their way in. Not only was she a well-respected name, known for her dress that so elegantly tied around the waist, but she was the President of the Council of Fashion Designers of America and could make all the right introductions to all the right names.

After some back and forth, they finally secured a meeting with her. They're in the car, driving along to the meeting, excited to once and for all sell their business model and secure a partnership.

And then, Diane von Furstenberg's assistant calls and says that Diane has to cancel.

Here's the moment that most of us would've panicked. I mean, I'd be banging my head against the steering wheel and dashing to the nearest Wendy's for a Frosty to eat the pain away.

But not Jenny and Jennifer.

Those two geniuses think quickly on their feet and go, "What? Sorry! We can't hear you! Bad service. . ." and hang up the phone.

And they drive right to the office, and the meeting happens anyway. And, well, the rest is history. (And I'm wearing a Rent the Runway shirt right now!)

How often do we seize opportunities? How often do we make our own?

Believe it or not, we actually make thirty-five thousand decisions each and every day—whether conscious or not.[35] Of course, many of these decisions are trivial in the grand scheme. Should I get guacamole today at Chipotle, or should I save that $1.25? Does this load of laundry call for two Tide pods, or just one? (I can never eyeball that.)

But, there are harder ones, too. Should I say no to a friend in need because I'm too busy? Should I send that email to my new potential employer because I haven't heard back in a few days? These decisions are heavier; you feel that in the way they sit in your chest. It's an emotional decision, so it's harder to decide.

And sometimes, a day will bring up opportunities that force us to make these tough decisions with limited information available to us. We may have to decide something that will influence the rest of our lives. As dramatic as that sounds, it's true. When these decisions crop up, all there is to do is lean into our own backbone and listen to our own intuition. Oh, and add a dash of courage and fearlessness.

I used to visit one of my hairdressers, Jena, at a salon in Denver, Colorado. She is immensely talented at what she does, has the warmest heart, and even offers wine to her clients when they get there (a little customer retention advice!). After going to her for about two years, she mentioned something to me about the salon's name changing to Mauve. I noticed changes within the salon itself, with colors and the general branding changing, but didn't ask too many questions.

Until I realized that she was the new salon owner.

She had been a contracting hairstylist when the same building was the former salon, renting out the chair space, and now she was the owner of her own business. People rented out from her, and she was continuing to rent out space from herself, too, to continue being a hairstylist.

I was totally impressed. She told me that news had been circling the salon for a while that the current owner's lease was up, but the location was perfect, and the stylists still wanted to work there. Someone had to step up to the challenge and take over, which meant entirely rebranding, re-incorporating, and starting a new salon that was totally separate from the former. Only Jena and one other woman at the salon, Amanda, were up for the challenge, which surprised her.

"When the opportunity came up, it just seemed like the next logical step in my career," Jena told me. They overhauled all the branding and had to come up with a new name. They settled on Mauve, appropriate because "Mauve" is a color (and they color hair) and shut down for a few weeks to make some changes to the inside of the salon to reflect their brand.

I asked her what the hardest part of this whole process was— as unique of a situation as it was—and she said it was the overturn. "Sometimes people are scared of change, and when roles are turned over so dramatically, and there's a new owner, it's a new dynamic." This contributed to a negative work environment, which was messing with the mojo of the new business—the last thing it needed. So, hairstylists began to leave and take clients with them. She said it's taken two years to get to a place where they're getting organic leads on their website, bolstered by Yelp reviews, and more walk-ins. But now, they're doing better than ever.

Jena's situation is also unique in that her partnership with her cofounder was completely spontaneous, and as she called it, serendipitous. The two of them stood up to take the opportunity and the challenge, and they were both admittedly hesitant about going into it with a partner.

There's so much to take from this story. First of all is the most obvious, that you have to get out there and just try. Jena believes that life is about GOING FOR IT, and I can get behind that! This opportunity fell upon two unsuspecting hairstylists and they took full advantage of it.

The second is, just because an opportunity makes itself available does not mean it's going to be smooth sailing—or that you even have to run with it! They had to learn as they went along and take a lot of advice from those in their circles who knew how to run a business, especially their husbands, who are both in real estate. It wasn't a simple salon takeover. It was a salon overhaul! But, being up for the challenge fundamentally changed their lives and enabled them to start a business of their dreams.

TRUST IN THE FLOW

Being open to opportunities is another way of saying: trust in the flow.

After starting Lit Without Limits, I had been playing with the idea in my head of writing a book and starting a for-profit company called "Girl Without Limits." It was a way to get more creative with my influence. The Chief Financial Officer of Lit Without Limits was also excited about the prospect of starting a new opportunity—something we could go into together because we had worked together so seamlessly on Lit Without Limits. So, we sat down together and started to paint the picture of what this new company would look like, what we would put out, how we would incorporate the stories and the backgrounds of women all around the world into this pinnacle of empowerment.

I was totally stuck on "Girl Without Limits," convinced it was The Name, but an intellectual property attorney told me that it was taken and absolutely could not be used. I was frustrated for days. The way my creative genius works is that often the title or a fragment of the idea comes first and the magic of it motivates the work. In fact, *Her Big Idea* as a title came to me before I even knew what the heck to write about.

I wasn't quite ready to give up on the idea of the book and the for-profit company, so I sat with it a while longer. "She Is Without Limits" came to my head next. It felt a little convoluted and I still wasn't happy about giving up the original name, but "She Is Without Limits" ended up shaping the company and the book.

Every chapter of my first book began with "She Is." There was, "She Is Learning to Love Herself," and "She Is Learning to Let Go."

The blog, featuring women's stories, used that "She Is" tagline to help them define themselves—telling stories like, "She Is a Mother to Triplets" and "She Is a Rockstar"!

This extended to apparel. Our first two lines were "She Is Changing the Game" and "She Is Hitting the Books." It was a way to personalize, yet unify women from all around the world.

It was a way to celebrate diversity but to bond over common experiences and common missions. The sheer opportunity that arose from this perfect set of circumstances—an already taken name, a friendship and thriving partnership, and the desire to take our impact FURTHER, led to the publication of my first book, "She Is Without Limits," and the beginning of my first for-profit company, of the same name.

These sequences of events in both Jena's story and mine are reminiscent of that Steve Jobs quote, which is worth restating. "You can't connect the dots looking forward. You can only connect them looking back."

If we start to think of our journeys as playtime, a chance to explore, to dive into what feels good, and allow opportunities to come along because we invite them, we've entered what I like to call "The Flow" of life. But, we're only open to opportunities if we've programmed our minds to recognize them. We find opportunities in accordance with what we WANT for our life when we put an emphasis on the feeling of what we want—for ourselves and for others.

CHAPTER 7

BUILD YOUR COMMUNITY

———

Seth Godin, thought leader and author of some pretty incredible books, including *Purple Cow* and *The Icarus Deception* is one of the many thought leaders who supports the notion that we are moving toward a connection economy.

In other words, our likelihood of success is dependent upon our "connection capital"—how many connections we have, and how they span outward, like a spider web that continues to span and reach further than we can see.

A notable quote by Dean van Leeuwen, another innovator, author, and thought leader, states:

The ability to form meaningful, emotional connections and relationships. . . will have as far reaching an impact as the industrial revolution had two hundred years ago.[36]

A notable quote by my mentor Deb Mills Scofield states:

The broader, deeper and more diverse your network, the bigger the impact.

And, a notable quote by yours truly, says:

Relationships are the spice of life.

Okay, so maybe my quote isn't worthy of making the Goodreads quotes page, but there's something to be said about the power of relationships, community, and connection.

In fact, Godin goes further in expounding upon this idea of a connection economy, calling it the "connection revolution" in a talk he gave at the ASUG Keynote at SAPPHIRE NOW.[37] He believes there are four pillars in which this connection economy is rooted: 1. Coordination, 2. Trust, 3. Permission, and 4. Exchange of Ideas.

We have to coordinate our connections and allow them to happen—whether organically, or through one person's pursuit. (Cold emails, anyone?)

We have to trust our community members, and those we form a relationship with.

We need to give others and ourselves permission to connect, to share, to bond, to learn, and to grow from one another.

We need to exchange BIG ideas.

To drive home just how important connection is, Godin posed the question: "The first person to invent the fax machine—what did he do with it?"

The audience laughed.

More and more every day, we are moving toward business models based on connected consumption.

Think about Airbnb. We are renting out our homes to strangers and staying in stranger's homes.

Think about Zipcar. We leave a car on the side of the road after grabbing our groceries that a stranger will soon use to drive to the post office.

Think about WeWork and WeLive. We are sharing coworking and co-living spaces, leading to higher rates of connecting and networking.

This is primarily due to the rise of social media. We're connecting with hundreds to millions of people daily on our platforms—many of whom we've never met.

In fact, we're now meeting people that have a pivotal effect on our lives via social media.

Take Facebook for instance. It now has over 2.2 billion active users. Think about those in your life you've connected with via Facebook. I scored my job because I met the cofounders of the company on Facebook. I met my best friend because I found her on Facebook before we both transferred to Brown. I met my BOOK COACH via Facebook!

I have near hundreds of friends and connects who I've never actually met in person, but I know via Facebook. And hey, when we meet in person, it's just as exciting as reconnecting with a long lost friend.

The Connection Economy is heightening its momentum daily; and you need to prioritize becoming an active participant.

When Jennifer Hyman, cofounder of Rent the Runway, started Project Entrepreneur with Jenny Fleiss, she said at one of their conferences that they started Project Entrepreneur because they felt that what they needed most but lacked while they were starting out was a "network of connections that could give [them] tactical advice."

It is now more important than ever to harness the power of community and lean upon people we can trust and confide in while we're pursuing our BIG ideas.

We should always be actively pursuing relationships with people we trust, who can share their honest opinions with us and introduce us to the right people when we need it.

It should be noted that these people don't necessarily have to be in our industry, in our geographic region, our age, or our experience level.

As Director of Community for Next Gen Summit, I've been holding what I've coined as "Power Pods"—whether at in-person events or over video calls, I ask random community members on Facebook to join in on a "get to know you" call with three other members.

I intentionally randomize this selection process. And, something really weird has started to happen.

When the members come onto the calls with people they've never met—people from different backgrounds, walks of life, industries, and experiences—they *always* get what they're looking for. Someone always knows someone else to help them or has that critical piece of advice, and such a propensity of epiphanies and further connections happen that everyone is left totally energized afterward. And, they remain connections, continuing to talk and offer support to one another.

So here's where I say: Don't discount the power of a connection, regardless of who it is, and how "random" they may seem. They may not be in the target market for your idea or have any "obvious" insight on how to help you, but to quote a childhood favorite, Bill Nye the Science Guy:

"Everyone you will ever meet knows something you don't."

So, go to the networking events. Set up phone calls. Send messages via LinkedIn or email. Aim to connect with as many people as you can, and ask for what you're looking for. If you don't know what exactly to ask, simply say, "Tell me about how you got to where you are today."

Asking for an advice from someone more senior is a great way to get the conversation started, especially if it's just a small nugget of advice that doesn't take much time for them to give. People like to feel like what they have to say and offer is of value to others, and that they're a "thought leader" or "mentor in their field." And make sure to include WHY you're in need of this advice. Studies show that people are significantly more likely to say "yes" to an ask if there is an explanation for why you're asking in the first place.[38]

People also like to feel like they're giving this advice to someone who truly cares about them and isn't in the conversation with selfish intentions. So, always, always, always ask, "How can I help you?" Even if you don't necessarily think that person is in a place where they "need help." Send yourself an email reminder if they mentioned they have a big event coming up on a certain day, so you can check in and wish them well. Sustain connections to the best of your ability, with your whole heart. Because, at the end of the day, the best connection you can have that will vouch for you the most loyally is a *friend*.

Next time you are in a large group, observe something very significant: the most important person present is the one person most active in introducing himself.

~ DAVID J. SCHWARTZ, *THE MAGIC OF THINKING BIG*

Sage entrepreneurs urge: Once you come up with an idea, tell EVERYONE about it.

First of all—our brains are connecting dots all the time. When we hear something that reminds us of a person, an idea, or a story that we recently heard, we connect the dots.

Have you ever been introduced to someone else who became extremely helpful to you, all because the "connector" of the two of you remembered what you were working on?

Me too. So, we increase our chances of being connected with more helpful connections the more we talk about our idea and what we're working on. Whoever we talk to will remember and be more than happy to bring you up when talking to someone you should be connected with.

The founders of DIY flower arrangement company It'sByU recall a time they went to a networking event, and Caroline (one of the cofounders) happened to speak with someone seemingly random about their company.

He called her the next day and became one of their first investors.[39]

Here is a tried and true list of the "types" of people you should make sure you have in your network as you venture into the wild world of entrepreneurship.

1. **An Actual Entrepreneur**. Or, someone who has done this before. This one seems a bit obvious. And I think you need about a dozen people who have "done this before" (the entrepreneurship thing) in your industry. They're going to tell you the honest truth about the target customer segments and allow you to learn from their mistakes. Are you starting a company in the retail industry? Great. Contact alums from your alma mater or peruse your LinkedIn for about a dozen other individuals in the retail industry and strike up a conversation. They don't necessarily have to be the Nordstrom's or Kate Spade's of the world—remember,

every connection carries the same value, regardless of how "powerful" or "well connected" they are.

2. **A lawyer**. My goodness, I cannot emphasize this enough. First of all, lawyers know other lawyers, so you'll have bountiful options for who can draft your contracts and explain to you the legalities of businesses. And most pertinently— everyone is going to need legal advice at some point, but may not necessarily need to hire a lawyer just to ask a few general questions.

3. **A Media Maven**. Someone in Public Relations or Publicity. Invariably, you're going to need a press release or some type of press attention when you launch. You want to be able to ask someone for advice on how best to do this for your company and get eyes on what you're putting out there—from the language of a press release to your marketing materials.

4. **A Certified MBA**. This one is a bit controversial, so take it or leave it. Regardless of the popular misconception that you can't "learn" entrepreneurship, MBAs are always going to have an astute understanding of business models and the market. You can always learn from an MBA—even if you're one yourself.

And about two hundred people you can list off the top of your head that don't match any of the above. Connections reach outward, like a spider web, touching people so far beyond yourself. Never underestimate what can happen by simply asking someone, "Do you know someone who (does that one thing that I really need)?" And, never underestimate how much YOU can help someone by offering them a connection to someone they really need, or even by asking for help. People like to know that their wisdom and experiences have contributed positively to others.

Communities make us stronger.

Communities buy our products, rep our swag, post about us on their channels, tell their neighbors about our podcast.

And the very, very best communities make sure we are doing the BEST we can in fulfillment of that BIG idea.

CHAPTER 8

WHEN AN IDEA
IS MAGIC

───

I'm often asked—how do you know when an idea is IT?

You know, IT. Like an idea that can be BIG BIG BIG just by the nature of its merit, that's so magical that everyone will swoon over it, that will make millions in year one?

If you take nothing else from this book, take this:

Your idea, no matter how magical the brand or packaging or company culture, is not going to retain its magic *if it does not solve a serious customer need or problem.*

Deb Mills Scofield is my mentor and teacher at Brown. She worked at Bell Labs for much of her early career, where she created one of AT&T's all time highest-revenue generating patents. She writes for the Harvard Business Review and was a partner at early stage venture capital firm Glengary LLC. I've learned much about innovation from her.

Deb uses Strategyzer value proposition canvases to exhibit how a product or service needs to solve a serious customer need or problem. Strategyzer is a tool created by Alex Osterwalder. Go ahead, make a free trial on Strategyzer when you're ready to flesh out your idea, and you'll see just how helpful it is.

A value proposition outlines a customer profile, in which we get to know our customers' jobs to be done, greatest pains, and gains. The ideas that work, and are magical, understand their customers' profiles greatest pains and problems.

Let's use Bumble as an example—the dating app. The customer profile is women, aged between eighteen and thirty-five, looking to find their next date. Their greatest pain is that they're having a hard time meeting potential significant others in their area, and other dating apps or profiles give men too much autonomy, so they're often flooded with forward, unwanted messages (Ahem, Tinder).

Bumble's founder, Whitney Wolfe Herd, was actually the cofounder of Tinder. Although she left Tinder for reasons other than the creation of Bumble, I think the difference between the two apps represents the value proposition and the necessary pivots well.

The value proposition canvas asks the entrepreneur to fill in the "gains" for the customer—and, as obnoxious as this is, we cannot fill in the details of our own product. The "gains" are what the customer will receive from the best possible solution out there. So, you have to get uncomfy for a second, and imagine. If the skies opened up and a perfect product or service came down from the heavens, what would it be?

Whitney must have recognized, "Hmm, actually, the perfect product would be a dating app where women message men first." This gives women more autonomy and control in the dating world. And thus, Bumble was born, and has been as fantastic of a company as it's been a fantastic product. (I got one of my best friends on Bumble and she's been with a guy she met on there for three years! Thanks, Whitney.)

Deb reminds us—it isn't our job to solve EVERY pain and deliver EVERY gain of every customer. That's pretty much impossible. So, we'll settle for solving the biggest pain and delivering the biggest gain.

But, keep in mind that every customer has constraints over when, how, and where they will use your product and service. Deb once was advising a museum that believed its target customer market was young moms who would bring in their children. They also believed that their main competitor was other history museums in the area.

Oh no, said Deb the Genius. Actually, your competition includes every other activity the young mom will take her children to in their time together. But, there are constraints here. Is it raining? Okay, the competition may just be the movie theater. Is it sunny out? Hmm, now you're competing with the amusement park AND the playground.

Deb conceptualized it in this way, too, so you can practice being a "consultant":

Your customer is hungry. Your customer is in a hurry. Your customer will be driving, so they only need one hand. Oh, and they won't be able to eat for a while.

First of all, does your customer want to eat?

(If you're anything like me, you'll be like, DUH! Who doesn't want to eat? But hey, we can't assume the needs of a customer.)

So say yes, they do want to eat.

Okay, they're in a hurry. So, they aren't going to Ruth's Chris Steakhouse for a romantic candlelit dinner. The options of what they can eat start to slim—maybe a popsicle, a salad, a hot dog from the hot dog stand on the corner.

Oh, but they'll be driving, so they can only use one hand (don't try this at home, folks). Okay, it would be really impossible to eat a salad with one hand. Maybe a pizza slice?

And finally, they won't eat for a while, so they want something that sits heavy on their stomach. Great—protein! A cup of yogurt. But, remember the prior constraints—one hand.

Before I make you too hungry, let's break this down. Every customer has different needs and pains at different times. There are always constraints on what is best for them at that moment. Better understanding our customer's constraints and desires, and when they'll come to us for our product or service, allows us to better deliver.

Clayton Christensen, a Harvard Business School professor, spoke with Sarah Green Carmichael in 2018 on a podcast and shared this anecdote:

McDonald's, many years ago, started doing a bit of data research on what products sold when, looking for a pattern of their most popular options, and how to diversify their selection.

They found that milkshakes, of all things, were selling like hot cakes in the morning. Why do you think this is?

The milkshake dilemma is similar to the constraints we just went over. A customer is driving to work at 8:00 a.m., and they have a long drive in morning traffic. They won't be able to eat until lunch. They only have one hand.

And, there are a plethora of foods they could "hire" for this very important job.

Christensen demonstrated:

Take my word for it—never hire bananas. They're gone in less than a minute, you're hungry by 7:30. Yeah, as you can say, I hire donuts a lot. I can never hire just one. But that creates problems on their own.[40]

You heard it here, folks. Never hire bananas.

So what is the solution?

Turns out, a thick milkshake gave them something to occupy them while they drove—something to sip on in traffic that would ultimately hold them over until lunch. In the morning, that was the milkshake's "job to be done." Later in the day when the same consumer picks up their kids from school and takes them for a treat, they may hire a milkshake again—but not for the same job.

Our task is to identify why our target customer would "hire" our product and service and capitalize on this. McDonald's took this critical piece of information and made coffee drinks like milkshakes—frothy Frappuccino—like cups of goodness to attract even MORE customers.

So, if McDonald's had lured in a focus group of one hundred with free Big Macs to ask questions about their purchasing habits and what products they'd like added to the menu, would the customers have said anything about the milkshakes?

Likely, no. Deb says, which I agree with—customers don't actually know what they want.

An idea is magic if you can anticipate a customer's desires and solutions before they even know what it is—and they aren't going to know what it is.

But, you can only do this if you get into the field and start to observe your customers.

Danny Warshay calls this bottom up research.

Here's a popular story to share my point:

P&G created Tide and were losing a bit of market share to their competitors. They had no idea why, so they got a focus group together and asked them general questions about the satisfaction with Tide. There were generic answers, nothing too clear, and they were still lost.

So, they got out "into the field" and watched people use their detergent. Yes, they sat in their houses and watched them do their laundry. I didn't tell you any of this was comfortable.

They noticed something. After pouring the liquid detergent into the washing machine, it dribbled down the side of the container, making a sticky mess.

They asked the Tide customers. "Doesn't that bother you?"

"Oh yes," they proclaimed. "It's so annoying." They took their paper towels and wash cloths and wiped it off. BINGO!

It should be noted that this annoyance was never once mentioned in the focus group.

So, P&G got hard to work re-designing the lid of the detergent, making it so that any residual liquid dribbled back into the container, rather than on the outside.

And, well, they haven't worried about the competitors ever since.

But once we get the solution and problem-solving element of a really good idea or a really good company out of the way, I believe there are extra, fantastical elements that add the "fairy dust on top."

The first of which should be apparent in its most formative stages: the universe/coincidences/the "world" seem to like it.

Ok, this one is purposely generic because it's dependent upon your beliefs about the world—if you romanticize the "meant to be," or what constitutes a "sign" to you. You have to follow what seems to be working. Do you share your idea with others who immediately want to be involved with it somehow? Does it take on a life of its own?

Back to Rent the Runway—on their podcast, Project Entrepreneur's #theTools, (which is a MUST listen!), they talk about the moment they knew Rent the Runway was going to work. They tested the theory on Harvard's campus, bringing an expensive designer dress to a college student and having her try it on.

They watched her twirl in front of the mirror, radiating with confidence, and say, "I look hot." [41]

That's when they knew what the purpose of their idea was— to democratize luxury. And that's when they saw that their idea was no longer just of their creation anymore, but its own entity—an idea that could literally be worn by another person, who saw and felt the same magic they believed it possessed.

When it comes down to it, the idea's magic is really dependent on others' perceptions of it. It may be something big, like when Kara Goldin, founder of Hint Water, realized Coke and Pepsi executives were asking to not be put on the same panel as her. So she understood who her new big wig competitors were. But it's also the smaller conversations. How easy is it to make progress on your idea? How fruitful are the conversations about it?

I believe that initial conversations around an idea should be easy, free-flowing, and seemingly serendipitous. This is part of getting into "The Flow." If an idea is supposed to come to life, believe me—it will. The people you talk to about it will want to keep talking about it, offer you resources, and get involved. Maybe you know exactly what I'm talking about. You heard an idea from a friend or caught wind of a new and emerging brand, and became totally obsessed with it. YOU gave it life beyond its role as an extension of the intellectual genius that created it. The entity, then, will have aspects about it that retain that same magic. Think about when you see the Walt Disney logo, which is Walt Disney's autograph. It's still magical to you. His idea to make a dreamland both on screen and in person became an entity separate from him that retains its magic to everyone, even after his death.

And, this brings me to the second indicator that it is, indeed, magic—the identity of the idea, paired with your creative genius, takes on a cult-like brand.

Have you ever heard of a company that has particular quirks that are so darn cute you can't help but think, ooh, I wish I'd thought of that?

Or, perhaps the brand and the company just seems to "get you." Ah, yes, that's no coincidence. They've done all the necessary research to "get you."

It can be as simple as the inside of the packaging you receive when you order a product from the company. My best friend Rachel, upon opening her first shipment from skincare company Glossier, squealed with delight at the bubblegum pink interior of the box with darling quotes.

Those little things matter and make you remember the experience of receiving the product. They make you open your laptop to online shop or grab your keys for a drive to the mall on the days you want a "pick me up." You remember that crazed consumer feeling, exacerbated by just-so-perfect messaging and colors and personality, and you gotta have it again.

Or, when you're all out of that last drop of foaming facial cleanser, you won't think twice about ordering again rather than going to another product, even if that other product is better! Yes, you read that right.

The cult brands sell a FEELING—a feeling of belonging, of ecstasy, of superiority as a result of having the product or being affiliated with it. And for that, they can set a price tag as high as they'd like, given that the feeling of euphoria for the customer is "priceless."

For me, my top-of-the-list cult brand is Drybar, the whimsical and chic hair company with high-quality products ranging from dry shampoo to leave in conditioner. (It definitely helps their cause that they're selling necessities—those types of hair products are life or death, people!)

I'm not totally going out on a limb when I say two of my favorite things in this life are blowouts and Happy Hour because, likely, you and/or fifty people in your life feel the same, and Drybar happens to touch on both of those. There's no thrill quite like getting your hair done (cut or color) because you feel like a brand new person when you go home thanks to the miraculous work of blowouts. It's enough to make me cut or color my hair way more than necessary! DryBar founder Alli Webb capitalized on the unmet need in her own community, realizing how many women felt the same way I do, wanting their hair done to feel fabulous to face the day. Oh, and they didn't want to have to cut or color their hair to get the blowout.

I'd already sampled a few Drybar products—enough to love the company and declare it my divinely ordained haircare go-to. And then, I walked past a brick and mortar location, mistaking it for a store for solely selling the products, and saw sign for the blowouts for the first time. Truly, that "No cut, no color, just blowouts" sign was all I needed to be sold. But then I saw the "menu" for blowouts, all named after cocktails. The "Mai Tai" for beach waves, the "Dirty Martini" for a tousled look, the "Manhattan" for sleek, and the "Shirley Temple" for girls under ten! THOSE were the branding message that took me from a potential customer to a cult follower because they were so clever and relatable that I wanted them all. And then, you get inside, and there are chick flicks playing on the screen! Did Webb know her customer base or WHAT?

So, I was happy as can be, getting my hair done with the "Mai Tai" style, sipping on Diet Coke and watching *Breakfast at Tiffany's*. You betcha, the warm and fuzzy memories of that experience will compel me to return again and again.

It's key to note here that, sorry to Suave and Pantene, I don't get that same fuzzy buzzy feeling with other, lower-price brands. No, the reason I pay nearly five times as much for my shampoo and hair products is because I'm in love with the feeling

Drybar gives me. It's the reason we prefer staying at the Ritz Carlton over the Days Inn (if we can afford it). We like feeling special. We like luxury.

I know I've been preaching that an idea is only going to work if it meets a need, but beyond the need to shampoo our hair and to have a place to stay on vacation, there is a real and tangible need to feel that we've treated ourselves and to feel like royalty. It gets the serotonin flowing and gets us addicted to the cult brand.

A key to creating this sweet spot—that cult brand—is to imagine the ideal world for your customer. I believe in many cases this means getting in touch with your own ideal world. If you're creating a product or service that matches an unmet need, you've recognized in your own life. Now, exacerbate it. Make it your twenty-first birthday party. Throw in some glitter and some balloons and make your customer squeal with delight and throw their credit cards at you. The best of the best brands have that magic touch because they're truly making dreams come true. They don't settle for solving a problem or meeting an unmet need. They want to make their customer gleeful!

You have your own Drybar or Glossier—that brand you swear by, recommend to everyone, or even selfishly want to keep to yourself. What is it about that brand? I think you'll find that apart from the obvious (it's a good product or service and does what you pay for it to do), it creates that dreamlike, drink-the-Kool-Aid sensation in you—that I need it, gotta have it, can't live without it one.

That's the magic of a great BIG Idea, in expression, as well as the independent entity it becomes.

CHAPTER 9

WHEN AN IDEA
IS *NOT* MAGIC

———

Have you ever heard the term "Love Goggles"?

How I Met Your Mother's Barney Stinson refers to these goggles of sensory misconception also as "Graduation Goggles." (Referring to when we graduate, become overly sentimental, and thus start to see everything with a rosy, "these were the best years of my life" perspective—a sensation I can absolutely attest to, as a recent graduate.)

These "goggles" of reality distortion happen when you fall head over heels for something and lose any realistic perception about what it really is.

Maybe you're infatuated with that new special someone in your life, and none of your friends can understand why.

Maybe you're infatuated with a new craze, like vegan smoothies or Soul Cycle.

Or maybe. . .you're infatuated with an idea. Which, for the record, isn't actually the way to go about entrepreneurship. Deb says: be infatuated with the *problem*, first and foremost. Seek to solve it with your idea.

The hardest part about infatuation is that. . .well. . .it isn't quite love yet.

It isn't necessarily rooted in truth, and your perception of the object of your affection is too rosy and hazy to be seen in its proper light. We become deeply attached, unwilling to see it for what it is.

First-time founders are especially prone to keeping their love goggles. And that's a major factor in the statistic that only 10 percent of first-time founders succeed. Our human sense of attachment to our idea and our company hinder our self-awareness, so we're less likely to take advice from someone who knows better, and even less likely to make critical changes and pivots.

The founder of Critica (a failed internet startup), reflected on his own attitude when Critica began:

> Most first-time entrepreneurs don't listen to advice very well. . . The trait that makes you believe that you can be the statistical anomaly is actually the same trait that gives you blinders when you are in the startup trenches for the first time. You think that you know it all. After all, you're already successful in your mind, so who cares what others have to say? **Fight that urge every day. . . You know nothing.**[42]

You're probably thinking—what? Am I still reading the same book? I thought this book's intention was to empower me as an entrepreneur—and hey, I'm *going to be a first-time entrepreneur.*

But, just because you're a first-time entrepreneur doesn't mean you're going to make the same mistakes as other first-time entrepreneurs. Knowing that love goggles are real and, well, you don't know much yet, will enable you to take a step back and prioritize self-awareness and a critical perception of your idea. And that critical perception might just be the magic twist that allows you to take your idea from your baby to a multi-million-dollar company.

I'm no stranger to this. When we started She Is Without Limits, I thought the idea was absolute MAGIC. I was in the creative flow, every idea that flowed from my pen to paper and in conversation had that magic spark. I remember thinking that even our logo carried the same regality as the Walt Disney logo. It was truly one of the most exciting times in my life.

I thought others shared the view of this magic. There was so much excitement surrounding the launch party, and it seemed that so many women were onboard with the mission. They were writing blogs for us, buying the apparel, posting pictures of themselves in the apparel, and recommending us to friends. Opportunities abounded! There were no limits to who we could collaborate with or what we could accomplish. It was the sparkly, fairy dust kind of magic.

One day at a startup fair at Brown, I began talking with a visiting mentor who had come to support the table next to me. He had his own venture fund and sponsored Nobel Prize winning science findings. In short, he had the experience to know what he was talking about. I was impressed with his presence, his words, his stories, and his experience.

So, we got coffee the next day. I came excited and prepared to spill all about She Is Without Limits, feeling this was my lucky break, and his connections and expertise would catapult us to the next level. But, he looked at me blankly as I began to talk about the company, and I could hear my own voice and posture start to deflate as I realized there was no spark in his eyes.

He was not seeing the magic.

He took a moment, and I waited with baited breath for his opinion.

"Honestly, I think it's kind of janky," he admitted.

Gut punch.

This was the first time I'd encountered criticism like this about the company, and a mere plea, "But it FEELS like magic" wasn't going to prove otherwise or make him change his mind. He had heard about the business model and the idea and thought it was janky.

But I am not one to hear a negative opinion and throw my dreams out the window. I also took into consideration—he is definitely not our target customer. So, what's janky to him isn't necessarily janky to our target customer. I was down for the next few days, but shook it off, certain that the magic still lived beneath the surface, and would be revived for the *right* type of customer.

Looking back now, I realize he wasn't just being rude or flippant or not seeing the mission clearly. I was a first-time founder, and hearing that my magical, beautiful company idea was janky was not going to fly for me. I was in too deep.

I learned in that moment that as much as we, as female entrepreneurs, lead with emotion, there is no emotion in a business model. It either works or it doesn't. And creating magic for myself as a founder doesn't necessarily mean that I'm creating magic for the consumer. The consumer can't read my mind or pick up an emotion off our website. It doesn't rise like fairy dust from the cloth of the apparel or jump off the pages of my book. As hard as I try, it isn't going to do that for everyone.

DOES YOUR IDEA SOLVE A PROBLEM?

Kara Goldin had a Diet Coke addiction.

I really don't blame her. I, too, have a strenuous romantic relationship with Diet Coke.

But Goldin was bordering on eight to ten Diet Cokes a day, and while I can't say I haven't done it, I have to say that's a *true* addiction.

It's an addiction many suffer from, and not just with Diet Coke.

Goldin was an executive at AOL and a mom to four. She certainly did not have the extra time or energy to be worrying about this addiction, nor how it led to her pre-diabetic state.

She knew she had to do something to save her health and her sanity because boring old water as an alternative was not going to sustain itself.

And, she had to do it quickly because it takes about two weeks to wane off a soda addiction.

So, she started to look for healthier choices such as flavored waters and found that none of them really fit the bill for an actual healthy alternative—between the bubbles, the fizz, the exotic flavors, and the vibrant colors of the water itself (health with a side of artificial dye, anyone?), none of the alternatives were really compelling enough to satisfy what she was looking for.

She began to experiment on her own. She sliced up fruit, let it soak in her water, and had created a seemingly simple new drink based on simplicity and health.

She didn't think anything of it until her mom called her to ask where she got the raspberry water Goldin was always drinking, because she wanted to buy some for herself.

And, today, that same drink is called Hint Water.

What's compelling about Goldin's story isn't necessarily that she started a booming business. It's that she solved her own problem. She wasn't thinking about business or entrepreneurship or profit margins when she dunked some fruit into her water.[43]

Similarly, founder Drew Houston solved his own problem when he created Dropbox. He was annoyed that he'd left his flash drive all the way in Cambridge—four hours from where he was working in New York City.

This problem-solving capacity made their ideas magic. *They were their own target customers.* And, in both of these cases, the target customer market segments presented massive opportunities.

They both made great products. But they were also both very lucky.

Believing that a product or service that solves our own problem will catch on and be successful out on the market isn't always true.

Even though we think our own problems are similar to those of our target customer base, that's not always true. Because, the truth is, those of us who pick up this book and read it— those of us who are always thinking like entrepreneurs and have high aspirations to start a BIG company with a BIG idea one day—well, there aren't that many people out there like us.

It doesn't matter if we fit the same age demographic, location, interest, you name it.

We aren't always like the rest. Some serious market research needs to take place before we slap on the "good to go" sticker and start mass-producing our product. So, before you believe that your solution to your own annoyances is the one and only magic and BIG solution, ask around and do some digging. Your future idea will thank you.

A new slogan in the entrepreneurship space is, "Fail Fast and Fail Often," and it makes sense. The sooner you recognize that your idea isn't magic, the better. Because then you can pivot, or start over again. You don't have to spend years and years developing. You don't get extra points for trying forever in this game.

So, look out for the ideas that aren't sticking and aren't magical. That isn't a sign that you didn't come up with a good enough idea or aren't capable of thinking BIG.

Perhaps that idea just wasn't ready to be born yet.

Perhaps the *world* wasn't ready for that idea to be born.

And even more compelling, maybe it's because you have a much BIGger idea waiting inside of you, demanding your time and attention NOW, and this is the world's way of showing you.

CHAPTER 10

LET'S GET THIS SHOW ON THE ROAD

The value of an idea lies in the using of it.

~THOMAS EDISON

A common misconception is that you have to know everything about business, have studied business in college, have an MBA, or the like to start your own company.

Part of that definitely makes sense. We have to know how to read and write to write a book, for example, or know how to snowboard to ever make it to the Winter Olympics.

But as a result of the insecurity that we don't yet have the knowledge or background to bring our ideas to life, many of us are left with BIG ideas that nag us and are begging to come to life, without the means to actually bring them to life.

If we waited until we're 100 percent educated and schooled on how to be an entrepreneur, then, well . . . we'd actually never start the company. No one can be 100 percent educated and schooled on it because there isn't a science to it. Some things are better learned as we go along. There is no teacher like experience.

As for the business part that eventually becomes necessary— fortunately, it's like learning to ride a bike. You will fall down. You will have to practice. But there are so many people nowadays who know HOW to ride that bike, have experience in doing so, and can offer your wisdom along the way. Many of them have written books that you can study in the comfort of your own home instead of dropping six figures on an MBA. The *for Dummies* series is a good place to start.

Starting an Online Business for Dummies is the book that Bree Cevaal had right next to her when we hopped on the phone for the first time. She went to my previous university, University of Colorado Boulder, and just started a fashion company called June Threads. She is one of the best friends of one of my best friends (best friend inception; best way to meet people you'll hit it off with) and, when I saw said best friend sporting unique, spunky, gorgeous clothing on her social media and shouting out to Bree and June Threads, I had to learn more. This girl is in college and a year younger than me (a junior in college at the time) and was not only starting a business, but creating products that people were LOVING.

I saw this from the outset, and I was convinced of a few assumptions—namely, that she was studying business in school and had all the tools and mentorship she needed right there in Boulder, secondly that she had done something like this before, and thirdly that she had a partner and/or a team helping her with the tremendous feat.

But, no, all she had was her *Starting an Online Business for Dummies* book.

It started when her boyfriend, who is now an NFL player, was a football player at CU Boulder. She'd go to his games and, dissatisfied with how typical jerseys look, would start to cut them up, thread them, and make them, for lack of a better word, "cooler," using the bare basics sewing skills her mom had taught her. They caught on and her friends encouraged her to make some to sell. It's a big football school and other girls would definitely want to wear the new jersey. This definitely planted the seed, but it wasn't until a few months later that she woke up one day and said, "I'm going to start a clothing company."

She reflects that no one saw this coming—even her mom will say that never in a million years did she see Bree starting something like this, but it arose organically and gave itself life. So, she came up with the name "June Threads," the logo (a hip version of the barcode you find on the clothes you purchase) and put in orders for fulfillment in addition to designing her own line.

She had to learn from DOING that there is so much you don't think about when starting a clothing company—from the tags and the packaging for shipment to the returns. And she certainly continued to feel that sense of naiveté—that "What am I doing?" feeling. To make matters worse, her first shipment from wholesale was full of clothes that didn't feel anything like her or reflect what she thought June Threads should be, and she had to put up some serious upfront investment to get all those clothes in the first place. But, she recalls that, when she received the first shipment and organized a photo shoot with her friends, she knew this was what she wanted to do for the rest of her life—between the chaos of four photographers, all the models, all the outfit changes, she felt totally and completely whole.

She knew she had found what she should be doing.

She had found her BIG idea.

June Threads launched in the last week of January, and when I was able to get on the site after class, I saw that most everything was sold out, which even surprised her. Here she was brand new to business and still learning the ropes, and she had started a clothing company while still in college that sold out on its opening day. Thanks to her vision, sheer passion, and of course *Starting an Online Business for Dummies.*

BE IT 'TIL YOU BECOME IT!

Let it be known, I am not a supporter of faking anything, except perhaps a charity smile when a well-intentioned pal cracks a bad joke.

I think authentic communication requires vulnerability, and I think the only way we can become the best version ourselves is to be as unashamedly OURSELVES as possible and not fake it for a moment—because it's a lonely place to be when we're not completely real with ourselves and others. Remember, faking can often create the *myth* of a big idea, not an actual big idea.

And yet, the advice I have continued to hear from female entrepreneurs, similar to learning as you go or the *Dummies* series, is to "Fake it 'til you make it" ("making it" being: becoming a success). This is a phrase thrown around in a variety of scenarios, and while the "faking" is antithetical to what I stand for, I believe it's nothing more than a linguistic error. It should be, as Amy Cuddy says, "Fake it until you become it."

I say, BE it 'til you become it!

As a founder of a company, long gone are the pleasures of being real and vulnerable about your weaknesses. You can't tell a customer, "Hey, I actually don't have a background in aeronautical engineering, but I THINK my team likely did a good job constructing your new private jet," or the like.

A customer doesn't want to know that you're struggling to keep the lights on in your tiny startup office or that your fifth employee just quit this week.

They only care about what you deliver.

So, "faking" has to come into play. Or, performing, whichever you prefer to say. It's an age-old strategy of pretending to have it together so others think you have it together so you eventually will have it together (or the semblance of such, which in this day and age, actually counts for something).

In the Project Entrepreneur #theTools podcast, Melissa Ben-Ishay, founder of Baked by Melissa, spoke about the humble beginnings of her cupcake company turned BIG.

She was a one-woman shop, making her delightful, signature cupcakes all day and managing the orders just fine until she received an order for five hundred cupcakes with an all too quick turnaround time.

Of course, an order like this would be "No prob, Bob!" for a larger bakery with, say, more than one employee. But Ben-Ishay wasn't about to turn this order down by admitting her lack of human capital to her customer. So, she pulled the most epic all-nighter of all time, with a flour tornado in her kitchen, and made every one of those five hundred mini cupcakes by hand. The customer never knew it was just her (but I imagine she'd get quite the tip if they did).

It's similar to Kim Kaupe's tactic when she and her cofounder began their record label, ZinePak. It was just two of them kicking along, but they knew most record labels have an assistant. So, they created an imaginary assistant, made her appear real by giving her an email address, and pretended to BE her on that same email while scheduling. No one ever knew, and it gave them instant credibility.

The reason I believe so wholeheartedly in BEING it until you become it is because something happens when you convince yourself you're faking it, or you fake it for too long. **We don't ever get to a point where we really and truly feel like we've become a success or become proficient at running our business if we've been telling ourselves all along that we're faking.**

The Imposter Syndrome is a serious factor. As women, we so often think we are undeserving of the accolades we receive or our accomplishments. There's a sense of, "Me? Are you sure?" We give up our power when we convince ourselves that we're imposters by telling ourselves to fake it. So truly, faking it until we make it is just giving ourselves the Imposter Syndrome.

So, we have to be honest and real with ourselves and those closest to us about how we're starting our companies. Being more open about the struggle and the constant learning curve will demystify the entrepreneurship world for other women, but also make it so that we don't feel as alone. I think the biggest misconception is that everyone else has it figured out. We see the amazing websites they create, their promotional materials, press mentions, and company growth—the highlight reels—but we don't see the struggle behind it.

And, just like the "myth of the big idea" that can happen with those who over project and fabricate their success, "faking it" places us in much of the same predicament.

You see, Ben-Ishay and her cupcakes and Kaupe with her personal assistant didn't fake anything. They rose to the challenge and became what they lacked. Melissa became a whole kitchen staff, churning out cupcakes 'til the sun rose like nobody's business. Kim became her own personal assistant. So that isn't, actually, faking anything at all.

We derive empowerment from stories like this, especially seeing how far they've come, with Ben-Ishay's national reach and Kaupe's accolades, like *Forbes* 30 Under 30. It humanizes the story of entrepreneurship and helps more of us "get the show on the road" without feeling that we're always behind the rest.

And remember—sometimes getting the show on the road just means making your product for yourself. If it solves your own problem, chances are it will solve someone else's. Start with what you have, where you are. Make what you can now, and know you have the capacity to bring it to life.

THE CLIFFHANGER

—

If we listened to our intellect, we'd never have a love affair.
We'd never have a friendship. We'd never go into business
because we'd be too cynical. Well, that's nonsense. You've got
to jump off cliffs all the time and build your wings on the
way down.

~ANNIE DILLARD

In January, I was accepted to a Fellowship called the "Scratchpad" by a company called Four94. You guessed it. It was named after the 2016 statistic that only 4.94 percent of venture-backed companies are female-founded (and they're named with the intent to make their name obsolete).

THE CLIFFHANGER · **159**

I applied with a business idea for an independent wine label that had been dying to be expressed creatively, but I didn't know the proper way in which to go about creating it. It seemed to be more of a creative passion project rather than something that could turn into a company.

It was a four-week fellowship, providing $200 for supplies, and it took place in January—conveniently over my Winter Break.

Four weeks later, I had created a prototype for my wine label with the help of mentorship and accountability, which gave me the courage and confidence to pursue it as an independent study for my final semester.

The founder of the fellowship, Risham Dhillon, was a great help to me, and I found myself wondering why she felt compelled to start this fellowship. I noticed that everyone else in it with me was a woman, and I knew this had to mean something. Everyone has a different reason or motivation behind starting something female-centric in the entrepreneurial space.

Risham and the Four94 team adapted the fellowship from entrepreneur Avni Patel Thompson's four-week test. This model: the four weeks, $200 model, appears to be the sweet spot for figuring out if one's idea really has merit before a founder opens a bank account and quits their job (or goes to other drastic measures) in pursuit of an idea. If within these four weeks, everything is going as planned and the market research and mentorship has been satisfactory, the risk has essentially diminished. Addition, Risham's team offers office-hours just for the purpose of "de-risking" situations to encourage more founders to jump in, knowing they have a support network.

If we're going to go headlong toward a big idea, it's unrealistic to just swallow our fear and pursue it anyway. And, the hard part about big ideas is that they often call for a major upheaval or lifestyle change (quitting your job, fronting your own financial resources, losing all your spare time) to accomplish. What Four94 is on to with this model, in tandem with the desire to make their own name obsolete, represents the push toward encouraging more women toward taking risks and therefore, toward the big ideas.

BUT RISKS ARE RISKY!

Remember in chapter 6, when I shared the wild statistic that we make thirty-five thousand decisions each and every day? All those decisions, in how we respond to opportunities as they arise, incur some degree of risk. We could potentially make the wrong decision.

Our *lives*, every single day, incur some degree of risk. Technically, we risk our lives when we cross the street, or get into a car, or even drink a cocktail from a restaurant that could be laced with poison. The reason we're able to live with all this risk and seldom think about it throughout our thirty-five thousand daily decisions is that we feel we have some degree of control over the outcome.

This illusion of control has been constructed by experience. We feel comfortable driving a car because we have driven for hours of our life—even if driving is potentially risky because we have curly fries in our lap (the ultimate distraction) and we're singing our hearts out to Fleetwood Mac's forever classic, "Dreams." Oh yeah, while it's raining. During rush hour. (To be clear: I do not condone this driving behavior!)

Contrast that with the level of comfort you felt the first time you were behind the wheel with your driver's permit at age fifteen, knuckles white, gripping the steering wheel as your parent or guardian prayed to the heavens above during your first drive on a highway. Scary stuff.

The reason that risks become perceivably less risky is because we did them anyway! We can't feel a degree of control over any perceivably risky endeavor unless we throw ourselves into it and *believe* we have a degree of control over the outcome.

A conversation with a female venture capitalist and Brown alum confirmed my research about how women are typically more risk averse.

I feel this, certainly, when I read Harvard Business School case studies. On reading the Eric Weston case,[44] in which he borrows hundreds of thousands of dollars, thus putting up his personal savings, a second mortgage on his home, a loan from his parents, AND a loan from the bank. I was sweating just adding up the numbers!

I cannot imagine putting that much on the line—or risking that much—for a company. But, perhaps that's because there is so much uncertainty when I put myself in Weston's shoes. *How would I know I could absolutely pay back the debts and end up cash-flow positive?*

(This is inherently problematic because venture capitalists want to see that the entrepreneurs they fund are willing to risk their own capital. After all, if they won't risk anything for their own company, why should the venture capital firm?)

The venture capitalist noted that if you tell a group of women and a group of men, "Go buy as much protein as you can with $20 from the grocery store," men would be in and out in a few minutes after grabbing some T Bones.

Women, on the other hand, would spend hours diligently searching the store, reading nutrition labels, ensuring they have THE MOST protein possible in that shopping cart. This attention to detail can certainly be understood in a positive framework, but risk and uncertainty aversion can cause more trouble than extensive time in a grocery store.

A study by Gary Charness examined gender differences in financial risks with investment portfolios. Charness' own research, supported by a number of other studies, "find[s] that gender is significantly related to asset allocation [and that] women's portfolios are less risky than men's.[45]

Investment portfolios make an interesting allusion. Similar to the financial, emotional, and time investment necessary to start a business, risking money in portfolios may yield great returns or great disappointment.

This risk aversion isn't because of an attachment to financial capital, either. Jianakoplos and Bernasek cite other recent studies about gendered aversion to risk, "[including] one by Brinig [1994], who found that women appear to be less willing to risk being caught and convicted of speeding than men, and one by Hersch [1996], who found that on average women made safer choices than men when it came to making risky consumer decisions, such as smoking behavior, seat-belt use, preventative dental care, and having regular blood pressure checks." [46] This is problematic because entrepreneurship necessitates a degree of risk because of the financial, emotional, and time investment that goes into a startup.

But another study by Rakesh Sarin and Alice Wieland added a dimension of explanation that clarifies some of these perceived gender differences, stating "Though our key finding that women are not more risk-averse than men for bets on real events is consistent across our studies, a hint of gender difference in risk aversion does emerge. Men tend to pay more for chance bets that are akin to gambling. Women pay more for bets on movie awards after controlling for their subjective probabilities, although the effect disappears when risk-seeking responses are excluded." [47]

In other words, women can mitigate risk if they feel they have some degree of control over it. They are less likely to play Roulette in Vegas, for example, but if they can strategize what they are betting on, there is no gendered difference with navigating risk.

The Affordable Loss Principle from Saras D. Sarasvathy's Effectuation Theory states that "entrepreneurs tend to find ways to reach the market with the minimum expenditure of resources such as time, effort, and money," which is the optimal framework for thinking about risk in entrepreneurship. The best entrepreneurs take advantage of the resources readily available to them and commit to this "bootstrapping." They don't necessarily need to "risk it all" in order to succeed.[48]

If women *are*, in fact, risk-averse, it persuades them more toward a bootstrapping approach. This is a great approach but limits their capacity to scale.

But, Sarin and Wieland's study may be more useful in understanding women navigating uncertainty—an entrepreneur does have a level of perceived control over the success of their business. This idea is in accordance with the Effectuation Theory as a whole, which is described as the "inverse of the causal."

Sarasvathy asserts that effectual reasoning "begins with a given set of means and allows goals to emerge contingently over time" and likens the process to "setting off into uncharted waters" (or into uncertainty).

He goes on to share: "the unexpected is the stuff of entrepreneurial experience, and transforming the unpredictable into the utterly mundane is the special domain of the expert entrepreneur."

To get this show on the road, you're going to have to go up against some risk.

But what if it hurts?

But what if it's scary?

But what if it drains my bank account, ruins my relationships, tramples over my credibility, and leaves me high and dry?

Thus is the name of the game, my friend.

I urge you to *instead* ask:

What if I *don't* pursue this one exciting, marvelous thing?

Because, what if it changes everything?

What if my life is never the same?

What if this experience makes me more ME than I've ever been?

What if I influence millions?

What if I MAKE billions?

What if I go down in history as the greatest founder of all time?

Because if the risky risks the *bad,* it should also risk the *good.* The best. The most brilliant.

And that, my friend, is worth the risk.

CHAPTER 12

THE TIPPING POINT

―

Ideas are driven by a single impulse: to be made manifest.

~ ELIZABETH GILBERT,
BIG MAGIC: CREATIVE LIVING BEYOND FEAR [49]

Katia Beauchamp and Hayley Barna are the founders of Birchbox, a subscription beauty brand, in which customers pay $10 per month for personalized beauty products. They recently created a model for men, too.

They had to start somewhere, and so their approach was well, to just go for it.

They didn't spend months thinking through the idea, getting

mentorship, trying to develop it to perfection before going out into the field.

No—instead, they started cold emailing their favorite beauty companies and bluntly asking: "What do you think of our idea?"

They didn't fully have the business model ironed out yet. But, the **simple ask** worked. They got their list of yeses and were able to go from there.

It was their tipping point.

Coming up with an idea, it turns out, is actually only half the battle. There is an inevitable lull that occurs after that idea is born. No matter how much you've thought it through, filled a journal with its ruminations, and talked with friends and mentors about it, there are serious operational considerations that come to mind when contemplating how to bring an idea to life.

One of my favorite TedX talks is called Programming Your Mind for Success by Carrie Green.[50] Carrie is also a female entreprenuer guru. She founded the Female Entrepreneur Association and has written many motivating books on women in business. And her genius transpired to this talk.

She begins by asking for a volunteer in the audience. You guessed it—no one raised their hand. Seldom do we ever volunteer for the terrifying and uncertain experience of getting up onstage in front of a whole audience when we don't know what the heck is going to happen up there.

Carrie expected this though, with a gleam in her eye. So, she asks again, and finally, someone says okay. He comes up onstage, she hands him twenty euros, and says, "Thanks! That's all."

Yup, he didn't have to do anything embarrassing or even address the audience. He just got a little cash. Where can I sign up?

She used this instance to demonstrate something we all know—we are TERRIFIED of uncertainty! It takes the really crazy ones to say, YES, we are going into this uncertain entrepreneurial venture. I may sink or I may swim, but I'm going for it. You either let that idea sit in your notebook and in your head, or you go after it with all you have. There is really no in between.

We have to take a bit of Katia and Hayley's spirit, starting where we are, with what we have, and figuring out the rest when we go along.

Or in the words of software guru Joel Spolsky, "Launch when your product doesn't completely suck." [51]

Sometimes good enough is, well, good enough.

So what is this tipping point? It's different for every person. When I first came up with the idea for Lit Without Limits, I had no intention of starting it anytime soon. I always knew, in the back of my mind, that I'd start a nonprofit someday, but a task that enormous seemed more appropriate for my thirties, or a time in the far distant future when I'd surely figure out the ropes with all the knowledge my older age would surely bring. Not now, not at age eighteen.

But, I became obsessed. I couldn't stop thinking about it. I was brainstorming about it in class and had already started to think of names, to Google the "how," to think through how I could do it. It had become part of my identity. I had to start it, and I had to start it now. If you're feeling the same about your own idea, but feeling stuck, this is your signal to START.

Start where you are, use what you have, do what you can.

~ ARTHUR ASHE, TENNIS LEGEND

May I add—you have to start even if the world is telling you not to. Once I decided that, doggone it, I was starting Lit once and for all. I began to seek advice from the leadership program at my previous university. Although they were supportive, I was told that especially in Colorado, there are way too many nonprofits, and I was better off volunteering my time to one that was already in existence. It's true; nonprofits are always in competition with each other for the donor's dollar. But, have you seen the juice aisle at the grocery store? EVERY product and business out there is in competition with something. I still believed I was not only capable, but created to start Lit, and I was going to do it one way or another.

The funny thing is that, once I started, I was asked often where I got the idea, and if I was seriously the first to come up with it. It seems like common sense to start book clubs with a curriculum and donated books with girls internationally—but **no one else** had done it beforehand. I took that as further confirmation that the pull inside me toward starting it was ordained by something greater than me, and beyond me. It felt like I was in the natural flow of my authentic self at that moment—doing what I loved, compelled by what I felt I was placed on this Earth to do, and this space of "the flow" allowed me to push past the obstacles and uncertainties that naturally arose from doing what I didn't know how to do.

How I got to this point seems to be totally driven by me standing on a ledge and deciding, stupidly, to dive, which may have you thinking, "Cool that it worked for her, but not for me." But the tipping point can be gradually tipped. You can dip your toe into the water and test the temperature first.

The same nagging, "pursue me!" feeling from an idea is a feeling Tiffany Yu knows well. Over two decades ago, she was in a car accident with her father that took her father's life, and caused nerve damage in her neck, forever impairing her use of her arm. This critical moment prompted what society deems a "disability" that she had to grapple with—not only with learning to live without use of her arm, but also for the great sense of exclusion that those with disabilities often feel.

The sense of exclusion began in high school when she was always the last to be picked on teams in PE. She recalls that this experience of exclusion, nearly universal in one sense or another for many, leaves a lasting impact on the way in which those who are excluded feel they can contribute to society. She went on to attend Georgetown University and began her company Diversability—a social impact company committed to rebranding disability through the power of community.

Afterward, she went to work at Goldman Sachs and recalls feeling her sense of self shift from her disability to that of her work ethic, sharing, "My work ethic transcended my disability"—a unique and particularly empowering feeling. She had noticed from her collective experiences that so much of the struggle of being in a marginalized group is living with the branding of other's perceptions. But in finding that her work ethic could transcend that, she found that identity can be comprised by so much more than disability. "I was not a victim of my identity."

And began the nagging feeling again—with the desire to revamp Diversability. The urge was exacerbated by friends and fans on Twitter, asking her what had happened to Diversability—a whole five years later. She figured this must mean something. If they're asking for it, that means there's nothing out there taking its place or doing the same thing. If there was still a need, there was still an opportunity. But, she had doubts about how much time she could allot. "It's a privilege to be in a position to have a passion project or a side hustle," she shared. Then working at music company Revolt, her time was entirely tied up with her full-time work and the responsibility of living in a city like New York City.

So, she took the "dip your toe in" approach. After sharing with a mentor and friend that she wanted to revamp Diversability, she was advised to host one event and see what it was like. This way, she didn't have to make any massive life change, like quitting her job or declaring to the world that she was a Capital E Entrepreneur. She could test her proof of concept and see what happened next. If it didn't succeed, she could shake it off and go back to life as usual.

Not only was the event a tremendous success (sold out tickets and all), but attendees were coming up to her after the event, asking what was next and sharing their excitement for its existence. Talk about a sign from the heavens! Putting your product or service out there and feeling the response is a great way to determine how much you should sacrifice now to GO FOR IT. Or, if you should spend some time ruminating on it, perhaps pivoting, before you put out another iteration.

But she knew it was time to pull the plug and go all in with Diversability as a result of both "internal and external" signs. The internal is that pull—that nagging feeling I speak of— that whispers in much of the same way the initial idea did, to go for it because it's time. And external factors, of course, depend on how much it makes sense on the outside. This does not mean her full-time job was going up in flames—in fact, quite the opposite . But she knew that she wanted to make a difference where it mattered most to her, to change the narrative around what disability looks like.

Since then, the magnitude of her success has been enormous. She was named one of the "100 Most Influential Asian Americans of 2017," a "Changemaker to Watch," one of "100 Visionary Leaders," and a "Woman of Influence." She's been featured in *Marie Claire*, the *Guardian*, *Forbes*, and the *Ford Foundation*, and her writing has been featured in the World Economic Forum, *Fortune Magazine*, *Business Insider*.

She spoke to how painful and uncomfortable it was to start to talk publicly about the car accident that changed her life and her family's life forever.

But sometimes the important work hurts, or is an overhaul, or takes from what we have now to give new life in the future. And with the community and new sense of life and inclusion she's created for those with disabilities, that very thought is coming to fruition.

But, the further you go down the rabbit hole of corporate life with a full-time job, the harder it becomes to leave to pursue a passion project.

There is something to be said for the amazing experience and business acumen you gain in working for a larger corporation, but it makes leaving sound that much crazier—and the tipping point for leaving to start your own business that much harder to tip!

Alice Kittrell is the founder of Outgift, an artificial intelligence program that tells you what the perfect gift is for your mom, your best friend, your neighbor—anyone. She began her undergraduate career at Rutgers University and had no real sense of academic direction. The one thing her mom did NOT want her to pursue was business.

Her mother was an immigrant and they had their own Chinese restaurant, which she had worked at growing up. Although her mom was an entrepreneur herself because of her restaurant, she told Alice that she didn't have thick enough skin to do business. And that's exactly why Alice applied to the business program in her sophomore year: to prove her wrong.

After graduation, it became apparent that the natural flow of graduates swam down the stream toward investment banking. She scored a job at Morgan Stanley in a role that supported the investment team, but she wanted badly to be on the investment team herself. So, she spent the next ten years mapping out her path to ultimately being an investor, jumping from job to job (including as an investment banker and a consultant), and even went back for her MBA at NYU Stern when she began to contemplate a career outside of finance.

But, upon her final year in grad school, she was given the keys to the castle she had dreamt of. She finally landed a role in private equity investment. Quickly, she realized it didn't get her up in the morning with excitement. So, as she was finishing her second semester, she took a class called "Entrepreneurship in the New Economy." She immediately fell in love with entrepreneurship. But she had already accepted her offer at a private equity firm.

This chain of events echoes another one of Doug Bate's assertions. The first time we think we've figured out our calling, we're usually wrong. We have to be willing to adapt and pivot based on what becomes more exciting to us as we go.

"Entrepreneurship in the New Economy" inspired her to start dabbling in ideas and building out business plans. That's how the idea for Outgift was born. Isn't it incredible how, when we're held in a cocoon of safety and therefore have the courage to start to think outside the box, we can be truly fearless? She had a job secured, she was following the "right way," and because it was safe to dream, she dreamt, and came up with an idea that she loved. She had created the emotional vision of her future self, and she couldn't let it go.

She had always found gift-giving to be magical when she was growing up and pinned her "dream job" as something that had to do with gifts. She saw the market need; we all know that a huge pain point in our lives is not knowing what to get for those we care about! So, she decided to go for it. She taught herself an algorithm in excel and hired a development team to create "Outgift 2.0"—all while continuing her full-time investment banking job, mind you.

She realized quickly that she was going to need to raise capital for Outgift. She was funding it all from her own pockets and needed the funds to truly scale the business and enhance the algorithm. But, she noticed quickly that "no one likes a solo founder." It becomes a Catch 22 because investors don't want to invest in a solo founder and almost always require a team, but it's nearly impossible to attract a team without funding. While trying to build out her team early on, she was often approached by interested parties looking to take advantage of her situation. In the midst of all of this, she had her first child, and postpartum depression made the hustle of entre-preneurship that much more difficult.

Alice was accepted into the Monarq Incubator in New York City—her chance to find a team, raise funding, and take Outgift to the next level. Alice is an example of someone who kept on keeping on, who uses adversity as motivation and chooses Outgift above all else. It's in alignment with her fantastic vision of the life she wants to live, doing what she was born to do. Despite following the typical route that seems predetermined for our undergraduate careers, she found an idea that mattered to her more—one that encouraged her to get up in the morning, bright eyed and bushy tailed. She's carried that passion forth to create a software that can forever change how we give gifts.

Our behaviors and habits move us from our current selves to our future selves.

We tell our friends about what we want, and they start seeing the same opportunities and sending them our way. It isn't overnight, by any means, and it requires consistency of vision with the compelled effort fueled by emotion, but it's how we start to pivot, or "tip," from where we are now to where we want to be. It makes the "dive" less scary because we're starting to play in the feeling, and letting circumstances arise organically. We aren't diving down head first. We're just peering over the edge and getting our parachute on.

If your idea is prompting this same tug, and it's in accordance with your euphoric vision of your future self, you're on the right path. Doug mentioned that we have to be emotionally motivated by That Thing we want to create, or we'll lack the initiative to go after it. If we're obsessed with the feeling conjured in our imagination when we picture ourselves doing That Thing, we're more likely to sign up for a business class to help us nail down specifics, start setting aside money as a down payment on initial inventory or listen to informational podcasts on the intended industry instead of our favorite songs on the drive home.

The tipping point shows up differently for different people and for different ventures—some compelled by extraordinary circumstances, and some by the small pull that becomes a tidal wave and demands action.

THIS ONE LIFE

There are also life-or-death scenarios that bring business ideas and companies to us. I am fortunate to be connected with many awe-inspiring people, but no one holds a candle to Cherie Aimée, a near death survivor turned influencer who simply just gets it when it comes to life and business.

Many years ago, she was a female tech CEO, at the height of her career and loving life. She had started her own tech company with her love for programming and development. She had just gotten engaged, was planning a fairytale wedding, and was highly esteemed by her colleagues and friends alike. Everything was perfect and then she was diagnosed with cancer—Hodgkin's Lymphoma—and had to undergo chemotherapy.

She beat cancer, but a mere eight months later, her heart stopped.

She went into cardiac arrest, which means your heart completely stops beating and grinds to a halt in your chest.

In the emergency room, they did five minutes of CPR on her, which didn't will her heart to start to beat again. So the team was ready to call the time of death.

But one doctor in the room—her doctor, who had been with her through cancer, said he wasn't going to lose her. He commanded everyone to give their all and do what they had to do to bring her back. They continued to do compressions for a total of ninety minutes to no avail and chose to put her on life support. She was in a coma for three months, hooked to an external heart—a machine by her bedside that she relied on completely because she had no heartbeat within her own chest.

When she finally woke up, she had to undergo several heart surgeries. One implanted a smaller and more portable version of the heart device that lived beside her hospital bed for all those months, a bionic heart. This little device kept her alive until the heart transplant five years later, and allowed her the independence to move around and live on her own in the comfort of her home, but enabled little else. She shared the additional stress and trauma of preparing mentally and emotionally for a heart transplant. Would she make it? How could she once again go back to the hospital? Her heart was transplanted for a heart from a donor, and she remained on life support for another three months. She couldn't walk, move arms, or feed herself when she finally came home. She had completely reverted to infancy in a physical sense, and she let the pain and despair of this horrific series of events break her down for those next three months. "What kind of life is this? Why did they save me?" She had ruminated and lost the will to live with the amount of pain and loss she had experienced.

But thanks to a friend and mentor of hers, Grant Cardone, who reminded her of her power, she was able to begin to create something new and start looking forward. She began to launch a personal brand.

"Starting it was like a fire that I had to pull out from the depths of my soul," she recounts. She could no longer sit at a computer and type. She had spent the last several years of her life in complete survival mode and didn't know how to commit any energy away from her survival. But she found the knowledge within herself, encouraged by Grant, to know that she could create the impossible because her story was the impossible.

She had come back to life after death.

This empowerment enabled her to see the millions of people her heart could touch, as long as she spent the time to turn all her energy into HERSELF to not only survive but to thrive. She recalls one of the hardest parts, learning to say no and to choose only what was best for her and what matched the vibrational frequency she was trying to match.

"You can't see it now, but I am capable of so much more. I no longer need your permission. *I'm here now to live.*"

This message to anyone who could doubt her or make her feel LESSER empowered her further, even though she had to launch the brand from her bed, still disabled. But one theme persisted—the ability to stick to who she was, to express it authentically, and to measure her worth based on her SELF, not how talented of a businesswoman she is.

We ascribe outer traits, experiences, and titles to our worth. She was a big shot tech CEO and founder, but these titles were stripped when she was in survival mode. The world stripped her of the only way she was taught to see her worth. She realized that it's more about who we ARE than what we do. She believed that who she was had more power than what she could do as a tech CEO, and the widespread success of her brand instantaneously proved this true.

"The power to move quickly through life and get more done is to connect from the heart," she told me. She never had to pay for press, she realized, because she was sharing a vulnerable story with such a personal narrative, and journalists wanted to report on her. She realized she was doing what no one else was doing. She was being authentic.

She leans on trust in herself. She told me, "You need to not only survive, but THRIVE in every area of your life. There will always be resistance and struggle until you *wholeheartedly choose to live your life according to who you are*."

Now, Cherie is the Director of Communications for ShipChain, an innovative tech company leveraging the blockchain to unite a 13 trillion dollar fragment freight and logistics global industry. She reflects on this and her promise to herself— her intention to touch one billion hearts with her life. She's returned to tech because she feels this unique opportunity and its team vibrationally aligned with who she really is—not just because it can look good on paper or make her millions of dollars.

She urges other women in business to understand that they need a level of courage and confidence that they haven't quite tapped into yet to make it through. Owning your worth in your LIFE makes it much easier to own it in business. The two are closely married, the same.

At the end of the day, she realizes she has been called to make a massive change. She said something that will forever stay with me. In giving suggestions for how we, as women and as PEOPLE, can do what terrifies us and be uncomfortable, she's realized that her mission isn't about *her*, but everyone she is going to impact.

Our brains prefer the comfortable.

Whenever we begin to endeavor into something new, something uncertain that makes us vulnerable to the world and risks it all, it's normal to panic.

But Cherie's belief that her journey was to create a personal brand that would help countless other people enabled her to push past the fear and the pit in her stomach, even in the most uncomfortable of situations.

"I've been called here," she reminds herself and steps forward into her true power.

And that, my friends, is the greatest tipping point of all.

CHAPTER 13

WHEN THINGS GO WRONG

I hate to burst your bubble, but even if your BIG idea is the very best idea of all time, and you're the very best person to execute it, something, as some point, is going to go wrong.

As frustrating as this is, it's best to know about what *might* go wrong before you begin. I certainly did not know what might go wrong. That honeymoon phase and those love goggles had me believing firmly that my idea would sail me to the holy land without any rough seas.

Cash is king in a startup. Your company may run out of cash for various reasons. Investors pull out. Your own savings deplete. You spend all the venture capital money before you turn a profit.

Your competitor may have an edge on you. They may have just come out of the woodwork, or they may introduce a new and improved version of THEIR product that blows yours out of the water. (Hence why it's important for your BIG idea to be a BLUE idea—Blue Market Strategy, my friends, or else it's just an IG idea, and what the heck does that mean?)

You will make a hiring mistake. It's inevitable. Adrian France hired an entire team of new graduates with all-star resumes, but they weren't a fit because many of them didn't want the long hours and low pay required of a startup. It led to a toxic office culture and a near death sentence for The Odyssey. And, Adrian is a genius. The company still went on to make millions.

Ah, yes. Team matters.

COFOUNDER TROUBLE

CB Insights published an infographic just this year about the top reasons startups fail. The third reason on there (after "no market need," and "ran out of cash") was "not the right team."[52] This doesn't always mean that you and your team have bad blood, necessarily, or that it can turn out totally dire with a wild lawsuit, but yeah, sometimes it does.

My story is obviously a perfect example of that. But my story isn't an anomaly. It's a common occurrence. And knowing that should help you with a few critical pieces of advice:

1. Do not go into business with your best friend or your spouse. It will cloud your judgement. (There are, of course, exceptions to this. Bluemercury founder Marla Beck is the CEO of Bluemercury, and her husband is the Chief Operating Officer. They work together daily, and they've made it work for nineteen years, even with three kids at home. I think the key is managing expectations. They've obviously forged a special relationship and communicate well.)

2. Do your due diligence on a thorough Operating Agreement when you file your articles of incorporation, so expectations and contingency plans are clear for all involved. Even if an article appears to be salient, make sure to double and triple check it with everyone who signs it. Law is sometimes hard to interpret, especially when you pull out the OA months or years later and brush off the cobwebs and don't remember the specifics.

3. If something is bothering you, address it head on.

There are so many reasons I've loved writing this book, and one of which is the sheer number of women I've met who had stories that resonated with me.

One, in particular, was the absolutely wonderful Christy Johnson. We instantly hit it off and couldn't get off the phone for over an hour.

She is a "serial entrepreneur," just like me, and I was intrigued by her story. After starting three diverse startups that went on to have three diverse lifelines, she is now the CEO of Artemis Connection and a course facilitator of creativity and innovation at Stanford's Graduate School of Business.

After graduating from Stanford with an MBA and a masters in education, she went on to McKinsey to do consulting work. But, she had an idea for an educational startup that she did with a partner who was just like a dear friend—they even had their first daughters only four days apart—and it was, by all intents and purposes, a "dream startup." It went on to be acquired.

There was another startup that she had in her mind but wasn't sure if it was the right time to start it. She had just become a mother, after all, and there was that urge to resign to the "SOMEDAY, I'll create this startup." She had just started a new job and was expecting twins, and her boss had hired her with coaxing words about how their company culture would be supportive of her impending life as a mother of three and give her the flexibility to succeed in the corporate world and have time to be at home with her children.

And then, chaos struck.

Her twins came seven weeks early, which was a total surprise and completely shook her to the core. It gave her this sense that life was out of control, but also set a fire under her.

"What am I waiting for?" she asked herself, and recounts feeling this urge to stop making excuses because in life there are no guarantees.

It was her tipping point.

The startup she wanted to create arose from a problem that found *her* rather than a problem that she found. When her twins were born long before their due date, her maternity leave was filed under a "short term disability," but management at her firm said she had violated the terms because it was premature (obviously out of her control). He stopped paying her as a result. She learned from this deeply personal experience that the modern workplace doesn't work for parents and called up a business school classmate for Stanford to do a startup to help to solve this problem.

Her classmate was well-known and a bit "famous," and Christy recounts immediately feeling that there was a power dynamic implicit in their relationship. In the midst of her personal medical crisis and feeling vulnerable and incompetent with all the medical forms and loopholes, plus figuring out how to she care for twins, welcomed small tasks that her cofounder (We'll call her Angelica to protect her privacy.) assigned to her.

Christy did the business paperwork, filed the LLC, and essentially everything else that needed to be done, while Angelica hardly did anything. She felt like she shouldn't say much of anything—of course, every time that two cofounders come together, they bring a variety of different assets to the table. In Angelica's case, she brought the social capital because of her relative level of fame and influence. Then, there's the sweat equity, or the capital from pouring your work and energy into something. Christy felt like she was on that side of the equation, even though things didn't feel fair.

But they had an equal equity split, 40/40, with the remaining 20 set aside for future employees. They hadn't discussed what would break a tie should anything come up that they disagreed upon—a critical part of putting together an operating agreement and starting a business with someone else.

Disagreements started popping up like weeds—mainly over her frustration that Angelica was doing next to nothing (not even picking her up from the airport when she came into her hometown for a work week) while she was carrying the load.

"There was a sense of dis-ease that, if I said something, she could run my name through the mud because she was the famous one," Christy shared with me.

This, the questioning of funds, and the classic "blame game" exacerbated her sense of vulnerability. Christy found herself being questioned and interrogated over how funds were spent despite surprising costs that Angelica incurred, including stays in luxury hotels which were then expensed to the company.

It's hard to stand up for yourself when a relationship has a power imbalance, and undeniably, all relationships somewhat do. In every professional relationship you enter, it's transactional. It's not like a friendship, a relationship, or family. It's rooted in what each partner can bring to the table, how they continue to bring it to the table, and how they can bring the company to greatness.

After Christy's company was finally dissolved, there was a sense of *now what?*

She simply hadn't been taught to cope with perceived failure—as many of us haven't. She attributes this affixation on the failure of it to the male teachers she had who were never quite as scared of failure or, if they were, didn't vocalize it. It's hard to feel that you've done anything BUT fail when a cofounder disagreement leads to the dissolution of a company. But is it really a failure?

Christy's story is deeply personal for me because it mirrors, in many ways, my own experience.

While Christy struggled with the fame and social capital of her cofounder, I struggled with the age difference and differences in financial investment with mine.

I believe the first six months of a startup tell you everything you need to know about it because the first six months are less about the idea itself (because the idea only started it) and more about the relationship dynamic of the team and the work ethic of the individual members.

It's when the ability to pursue the idea is put to the test:

HOW is it going to be accomplished?

Who has what contacts to make it happen?

What day-to-day operations will each individual be responsible for?

There is so much to iron out and to discover—from market research to simply navigating how to get business going—that the stress and confusion can really culminate and put relationships under a steam cooker.

You have to feel seen and heard in a partnership. Once communication gets funky and lines get blurred, it gets really easy to find pent up anger and tension against the other person. I really believe now, in retrospect, that some of my own falling out with my cofounder could have been diffused if I had communicated how I felt sooner.

The truth was that the magic of my business had been completely trumped by the toxicity of the relationship, where I felt my hands were tied.

It started to break me down.

I knew I deserved better, but I felt fear around giving up.

The name of the company was the name of my first book. It was an extension of the first act of love I'd ever put out into the universe—my nonprofit—and I was scared that walking away from it would mean that I was also walking away from the biggest part of myself. I didn't know what was next.

Even the greatest and most magical of ideas can be poisoned by a bad relationship with a cofounder. Ultimately, fingers can be pointed and blame will be given, but the compatibility is where it begins. We are all disposed to spark arguments, heated debates, and misunderstandings with those we work with.

It's hard to have smooth sailing because starting a company is one of the craziest and most life-changing things you can do, aside from having a baby—and we all know that new parents don't exactly have a walk in the park in those sleep-deprived and chaotic early days.

That's why it's so critical to manage expectations, stand up for yourself, and never let communication fall by the wayside. If it's not working, fix it, and if it can't be fixed, get out. You may be able to continue the idea on your own or maybe another idea, untainted by the drama of a bad cofounder relationship, will come to you. But you owe it to yourself to GET OUT and never let a bad ending determine how you see yourself as a failure.

AND . . . MISCELLANEOUS OTHER REASONS

No market need, lack of cash, cofounder disputes, and more. All of these obstacles can easily arise and will. They aren't the only sharks in the water, either.

But the most well-developed business models with the greatest teams can navigate these challenges.

And, that's you and your idea. I promise you.

But sometimes, even then, life can and will get in the way.

Many years ago, my boyfriend's mom and her friend started a basket service to send gift baskets to college students within Colorado—a perfect gift for a parent, neighbor, or family member wanting to make sure their loved one has all they need up in the dorms.

It was a hit.

News of the baskets spread like wildfire and soon their materials alone were taking over her friend's basement. They reached a point where they had to decide whether to cease operations because it had gotten a bit TOO big for her current space, or lease out a space to have the room to fulfill the abundance of orders.

At this critical juncture, the Columbine High School shooting occurred, and her daughter was a student there at the time. While her daughter was physically fine, the horror of the tragedy rocked their community.

"It sent all of us into reflection mode, and my first priority was to be there for my daughter," she shared with me.

They chose to cease operations once the dust settled because she had lost the desire to continue.

She apologized while telling this story, worrying that it wasn't necessarily inspirational.

On the contrary.

I told her, and I truly believe, that we have to get real about times that life gets in the way. Entrepreneurship doesn't happen in a vacuum. Our ability to lead, make choices, and invest our time, money, and resources into a company is heavily dependent on outside circumstances.

But, if we can make entrepreneurship and the act of starting a company seem more like "play" that's subject to be shifted, molded, moved, and even ceased in correspondence with life, and we can take out the perception that things went wrong and therefore we are a failure, then we encourage those who are considering pursuing their big idea.

Elizabeth Gilbert asks in *Big Magic*, "What do you love doing so much that the words failure and success essentially become irrelevant?"[53]

If you love the pursuit of your big idea and love this adventure of entrepreneurship, give yourself the space, the freedom, and the respect to let go of your idea, should you need to. To put it on hold. To set it aside. To give it away to a new owner. To sell it.

Just as it came to you as its own entity, and you gave it life and purpose and meaning and color, you can set it free.

But just because things go wrong doesn't mean you have to.

It's in your hands.

Your big idea is yours, as long as you want it to be.

CHAPTER 14

FAILING 'UP'

Our greatest glory is not in never failing, but in rising every time we fail.

~ CONFUCIUS

Ah, the big *F* word.

We began this book with the statistic that 90 percent of start-ups fail.

And yet, I urged you to choose the pursuit of a BIG idea. Even in the face of potential failure.

Jessica Ekstrom is the founder of Headbands of Hope, an online shop where a customer can purchase a headband and have one donated to children with cancer. When she first began the venture, she was a junior in college at North Carolina State University.

She had just received a $10,000 loan to have her first line of headbands manufactured. So, she wired the money to the manufacturer.

And never heard anything.

And never received anything.

She was obviously horrified. My own jaw dropped when she told me this story. "I remember thinking, maybe this is a sign from the universe that I'm not supposed to do this," she recounted to me.

But, she knew that the reason she started Headbands of Hope was because it solved a problem. It enabled cancer patients who had lost their hair to chemo to accessorize without hiding their experience. No one else had created something like this before. And she knew, if her business failed, the problem would not be solved.

She recognized that this horrific moment could either be a call to the end, or a bump along the way.

She chose a bump along the way.

Brands and Fernandez-Mateo state in a Harvard Business Review article titled, "Women Are Less Likely to Apply for Executive Roles If They've Been Rejected Before" that: "Women are not only dramatically underrepresented in executive jobs, but they often encounter negative stereotypes about their leadership abilities in these positions... [those] pursuing executive roles are likely to have had direct or vicarious experiences with this unequal gender treatment over the course of their careers, and these experiences will affect their answers to the question, "*Do people like me belong here?*"[54]

Jessica shared that she used to believe that her failures were about her and her self-worth—as if entrepreneurship was a "roller coaster she wasn't tall enough to ride." But, then she chose to recognize that all missteps result from trying to make a change in the world. It's just a natural part of the progression.

If it had been easy, that would've meant the road was paved and someone had done it before her.

What a revolutionary way to look at failure.

Instead of giving up, she received a $300 grant from her university and used that small amount of seed money to go to a new manufacturer and bootstrap her way back up. She repaid the $10,000 loan eventually. And, because she didn't allow a failure to bully or taunt her into retreating and giving up, more than ten thousand headbands have been donated to girls battling cancer.

As I shared in the beginning of this book, my perceived failure after the crash and burn of my first company led to insecurities about my capacity to be an entrepreneur.

I began to have serious doubts about whether I belonged in the driver's seat of a company.

Did I belong in the "entrepreneur" club? Did I deserve to be a leader? Did I deserve to write about my experiences?

While these findings do not necessarily entail that women internalize rejection as a blanket fact or assumption, Geoffrey Cohen and Julio Garcia analyze that "when belonging, uncertainty is heightened, individuals pay particular attention to any cue that may inform their concerns, by signaling their acceptance in or exclusion from the domain in which their belonging uncertainty arises." [55]

In other words, it's human nature to look for clues to confirm that our suspicions about our place in the world are true.

Rather than pushing through and not accepting "no" for an answer, there's a tendency for us to use these confirmations as excuses to *stop ourselves.*

Kathryn Minshew, the founder of The Muse, gave a compelling speech in which she promulgated to *not take a "no" personally* (just shake it off!) and to perceive a "no" as a "wait a little." This reframing of the "no" is powerful because the internalization of rejection may be the reason that women *think small.* They're scared to think big because if they try and fail, what will that say about their worth?

Kathryn's overarching message in her talk was that if we're able to trace the success stories of female founders to their mentalities, maybe we can chart a new course in female entrepreneurship. We can teach mentalities in the same way we teach spreadsheets or competitive advantages.

I was afforded the exciting opportunity to plan and host the WE@Brown (Women's Empowerment through Entrepreneurship) Conference on March 3rd, 2018 at Brown University. Brown alumnus and Chief Marketing Officer of Popsugar, Anna Fieler, gave an incredible keynote speech called "In the Driver's Seat," in which she shared lessons she had learned over the course of her own life. It gave testimony to the old adage, "Hindsight is 20/20."

One of the biggest points that stuck with me was her reflection on her time as a caller for donations to Brown from alumni—a student job on campus is to call Brown alums and ask them to donate to the school. This was her job while on campus. She said, "I got a lot of *NOs*—sometimes, dozens of *NOs* in an hour.

. . . But, it made me realize a no is just a no."

Mic drop. (Not literally. Thankfully, she held onto her mic.)

Women are considered to be intuitive, deeply feeling emotions. It's not as easy for us to shake off the "no" and try again with a new vengeance.

Thus, my encouragement is to demystify the "no." Gut it, and make it less intimidating by diving headfirst toward it and wanting it more than we want the yes because it means we tried and learned, and now get to try again in a new way. Sheryl Sandberg shares the same sentiment, urging in *Lean In*, "Women need to shift from thinking 'I'm not ready to do that' to thinking 'I want to do that, and I'll learn by doing it.'" [56]

FAILURE IS REDIRECTION

Chaya Cooper, tech founder of Click2Fit, gave me a piece of advice for my own situation that really summed it up—we have ALL trusted the wrong person or been screwed over at some point by someone—in a company, in a relationship, in a friendship, you name it—but that's okay, because we often learn even more from failure than from success. And that's especially true of some of the skills most important for business success—trusting your gut, empowering your team (to both succeed and fail), engendering trust, perseverance, and an ability to recognize your own mistakes and learn from them.

In short, by going out there, knowing full and well that we're going to make mistakes and trust the wrong people and end up with somewhat of a failure, but embracing that and building who we are on resilience rather than success. And it's true—resilience is central to entrepreneurship.

If we start to see failure as, well, not a failure, but a fork in the road leading us elsewhere, we can shake off the heavy internalization of it and turn instead to gratitude for all that we've learned. Every time we do something wrong or something turns out in a less than satisfactory fashion, our "spidey senses" or intuition is sharpened for next time. We will know when something didn't quite fit, or when we shook off frustrations thinking it would get better. Regret shouldn't plague us; it should just be a roadmap for how to deal with similar circumstances next time or avoid them altogether.

If we remember the story of Sara Blakely and Spanx, you may recall that she took the LSAT in the hopes of attending law school and totally bombed it. She knew no respectable law school would let her in with a score like that and she was absolutely crushed by her perceived failure. But, turns out that LSAT was just a blip on her radar once she came up with Spanx and started a business. It was a blessing in disguise—Blakely may just as well be sitting in a law firm today, sending off some emails, and the world may not have Spanx, and she may have never tapped into her truly awe-some power to create something big.

When we look back at our lives after a good amount of time, we either laugh at what we thought was a failure or thank the situation.

Something else I took from failure is the recognition that, whoa—my worst-case scenario happened, and I made it through. I'm still surviving and thriving. I handled it, even though I thought I couldn't, and I'm better for it now. When I came to this realization, it became my new goal to ensure other women don't go through the same because they're armed with more knowledge than I was. Thus, I began an entrepreneurial incubator at Brown for female students with ideas, providing them with workshops, resources, and speakers to help them bring their ideas from concept to reality. I get to teach everything I wish I could have taught myself a few years ago, which deters many feelings of failure.

And, even more miraculously, I've found that I feel more fulfilled from creating and teaching this incubator in my quest to empower women than I ever did in She Is Without Limits, even though that was the central intention of the company.

Brandon Labella, author of the book *The Journey to Failing Freely*, put it best in a conversation with me about failure.

He told me that he believes "if you fail, the journey is more fulfilling." As wild as that sounds, it's so true. To be able to turn my mistakes into someone else's success and to be able to reflect on what I know now marks clear milestones in my entrepreneurial path. And I'm all the more fulfilled for it.

No one ever really learns anything from succeeding. Even when successful founders and leaders speak of their success, their acuity in framing it is informed by past failures. When we begin to see that failure is what adds the depth and inspiration to our journeys, we may not run away from it anymore. In fact . . . we may chase it.

So, with these new insights about failure, I have to say—you can't be scared of it.

You have to actively pursue it.

You have to learn by doing, but know that you'll learn even more than failing. No matter what happens, though, please don't fall prey to the belief that a failure determines your worth. Too many of us do this—men and women alike—and we can't keep experiencing and learning if we're scared that it's going to mean something about who we are if we don't quite get it right the first time. And if we choose to stop, and let what happened to us once determine more than it should, there's a big chance we won't give life to the BIG idea brewing inside of us, ready to show the world why we failed in the first place—to make room for the new.

Sophia Amoruso wrote so eloquently: "When you approach everything as if it's a big, fun experiment, then it's not that big of a deal if things don't work out. . . There are secret opportunities hidden inside every failure." [57]

Shaking off failure, even when it's as monumental and public as hers was, can be as easy as taking a lesson and moving forward. So, if we apply Deb's phrase, "Experiment—Learn—Apply—Iterate," then failure isn't failure at all. It's just the learning phase. We'll apply what we learned, and then we'll iterate.

There is also the type of "failure" that seems to arise when a company fizzles out. It doesn't face severe adversity, nothing "happens," per se, but the founder just feels as if it's run its course. It's time to move on.

Recently, at an event in LA, I spoke with a wonderful woman named Karen who had a fashion startup in her high school days.

She had started it with her sister, built the website on her own, and brought the clothing to several popup shops around her hometown in Virginia.

Eventually it just . . . fizzled out. She admitted to me, "I miss it." But, as she continued to talk about it, I realized that the role it played in her life was so much bigger than the fact it had ceased operations.

"It's the reason I moved to LA," she confided. "Even though it isn't what I'm doing anymore, it's made me who I am, so I'm forever thankful to it."

Goosebumps. Having the awareness that the many seasons and creations of our life can amount to our personal development and the natural expansion of our life's experience takes a level of astuteness, surely. She could easily view its now nonexistence as a failure, but she chooses not to.

Our "failures" are dependent upon our perceptions of them, and how we let them determine, or not determine, our narratives.

Seth Godin posits failure in an interesting, almost convoluted way. He doesn't believe that we are actually afraid of failure. Just like the age-old adage, "There's nothing to fear but fear itself," Godin calls it "the fear of the fear of failure." [58]

Jack Kaminski got to the heart of Godin's suggestions by stating in a LinkedIn article: "What we are afraid of is having to admit to ourselves that we did something that didn't work. Just remember, if you do not put your artistic creation out there, you've already failed before even being in a position to fear its outcome." [59]

All we have to give this world is what we create. If we rob ourselves of the chance to come up with a BIG idea, and to bring it to the world in a way only we can, with our unique vision and creativity, we have failed at the one big and beautiful task in this life: To give of ourselves and our talents in a way that benefits others.

So what if we fail? We only have one life. We deserve to try...then try again. And maybe even again. Because every time we try and fail, we are learning more about ourselves, creating more to give to the world, and creating an ultimately more-fulfilling life-experience for ourselves.

If you want to talk about BIG, it's BIG enough to scare failure out of its boots.

CONCLUSION

———

This wasn't a book about failure, after all.

This was a book about beginnings.

And so, "What's next?" is going to be different for every reader.

We have all arrived here, to this book and this moment, with a unique set of circumstances—how we were raised to see ourselves, how we have interacted with male entrepreneurs and venture capitalists, how we have tried and failed or not tried at all.

How we have imagined ourselves as the creators of BIG ideas throughout these chapters.

How we have grappled with our lack of ideas, or feelings that we aren't capable enough of bringing them to life in this world.

As individual as the pursuit of big ideas can feel on the isolating path of entrepreneurship, we are empowered in the collective when we share in our vulnerabilities and encourage one another.

I've found that there is no greater strength, especially as I reflect upon the first several years of my entrepreneurial journey, than that of the next generation of women coming together and holding each other in the belief that we can all create something that changes this world.

Celebration of stories of women who have succeeded in entrepreneurship can demystify the myth that entrepreneurship is inherently masculine. Debunking the no and deciding to be real and vulnerable about our interactions and experiences with failure can make failure seem less daunting. Emphasizing what COULD be can make our ideas seem more worthwhile to pursue.

We have to get the risk out of the equation by re-conceptualizing it and remembering that *we* are the ones with control over how our lives pan out.

Some circumstances are beyond us—this I won't deny. We don't know how our ideas will change. We don't know how they'll change us. We don't know how they'll change the world.

All we can do is trust that our BIG idea is worth pursuing.

We owe it to ourselves to look terror in the eye and say, "You are the friend of circumstances that I have outgrown."

We owe it to ourselves to allow whatever sense of the "impossible" that protrudes our optimism and breathes heavily on our back to fade away.

We owe it to ourselves to command what was once "just an idea" to reveal itself in its earthly form.

Only we can give out ideas the meaning, the flavor, and the sparkle they need to become more than ideas.

We simply have to trust that what was once merely an emotion—that ecstasy associated with a BIG idea—can become a marketable, sellable product.

That what we create is worthy of life.

That what we create is worthy of being here.

And, the craziest of all, that what we create is worthy of others' time, usage, their income.

That it can change how people live their lives, how they start their days, how they engage with others.

Whatever wild dream causes your heart to stir can come forth because of your own creativity and vision. It is magical because it is yours.

I hope that, in some ways, these stories and this book have been life-changing to you; because it is motivated by my own story: a girl with a BIG idea who threw herself into the pursuit of it and saw the fabric of her purpose mold and shift with more vibrancy than ever in the magnificent journey that unfolded.

Through the hard times, the failure, and the "get back up again."

To quote the incredible Amy Cuddy: [60]

"I am larger, better than I thought, I did not know I held so much goodness."

Go and get your BIG idea.

ACKNOWLEDGMENTS

Thank you to every woman who shared her story and her advice to make this book authentic, vulnerable, and real.

Thank you to my parents, who have encouraged my love for creativity and writing for as long as I can remember. You push me to be more of who I was born to be, and remain the unwavering cheerleaders of all of my pursuits and passions.

Thank you to Eric Koester, who supported my vision for this book before the pages were filled, through every moment of self-doubt and every epiphany. You urge me to prioritize creating and have helped me to find my authentic voice.

Thank you to Danny Warshay, who taught me how to think big about innovation and entrepreneurship. Your class has forever changed how I view the world and what I can create within it.

Thank you to Deb Mills Scofield, who gives her whole heart to her 'blue lobsters'. Your mentorship has shifted my sense of self and understanding of innovation; I feel forever grateful to know you and learn from you.

Thank you to Christy Johnson, who I met because of this book, and who has become an everlasting friend. Our friendship is a testament to the sisterhood of entrepreneurship.

Thank you to Doug Bate, whose support and life lessons have been revolutionary. Thank you for going above and beyond as a guide and mentor to me; I draw on your wise lessons daily.

Thank you to Brown University faculty members Hamzah Ansari, Drew Walker, and Sharon Krause, who encouraged me in my research and believed in the importance of my project.

Thank you to Justin Lafazan and Dylan Gambardella, for empowering me every day both as a woman and a leader. I feel so fortunate to work alongside men who believe in all my ideas.

Thank you to my best friends: Rachel Gross, Emma and Zoe Butler, Stephanie Reyes, Olivia Simmons, and Rima Reddy. You cheer me on endlessly, are there for me on the bad days, lift me higher on the good days, and make me laugh through it all.

Thank you to Nate Hummell, who celebrates all my endeavors, no matter how big. You share the same excitement for creativity, imagination, and self-expression; I love creating with you, bouncing ideas off of you, and reveling in your intellectual acuity and curiosity.

Thank you.

APPENDIX

INTRODUCTION

1   Ball, Sheryl, Catherine C. Eckel, and Maria Heracleous. "Risk Aversion and Physical Prowess: Prediction, Choice and Bias." *Journal of Risk and Uncertainty* 41, no. 3 (2010): 167-93. doi:10.1007/s11166-010-9105-x.

2   O'Neal, Elizabeth E., Jodie M. Plumert, and Carole Peterson. "Parent–Child Injury Prevention Conversations Following a Trip to the Emergency Department." *Journal of Pediatric Psychology* 41, no. 2 (2015): 256-64. doi:10.1093/jpepsy/jsv070.

3   Morrongiello, Barbara A., and Theresa Dawber. "Parental Influences on Toddlers' Injury-Risk Behaviors: Are Sons and Daughters Socialized Differently?" *Journal of Applied Developmental Psychology* 20, no. 2 (June 1999): 227-51. https://www.sciencedirect.com/science/article/pii/S0193397399000155.

CHAPTER 1

4   Kim, W. Chan., and Renée Mauborgne. *Blue Ocean Strategy: How to Create Uncontested Market Space and Make the Competition Irrelevant.* Boston, Massachusetts: Harvard Business Review Press, 2016.

5   Ertac, Seda, and Mehmet Y. Gurdal. "Deciding to Decide: Gender, Leadership and Risk-taking in Groups." *Journal of Economic Behavior & Organization* 83, no. 1 (June 2012): 24-30. doi:10.1016/j.jebo.2011.06.009.

6   Sundheim, Doug. *Taking Smart Risks: How Sharp Leaders Win When Stakes Are High.* New York: McGraw-Hill, 2013.

7   Lufityanto, Galang, Chris Donkin, and Joel Pearson. "Measuring Intuition: Nonconscious Emotional Information Boosts Decision Accuracy and Confidence." *Psychological Science* 27, no. 5 (2016): 622-34. doi:10.1177/0956797616629403.

8   Teare, Gené, and Ned Desmond. "Announcing the 2017 Update to the Crunchbase Women in Venture Report." TechCrunch. October 17, 2017. https://techcrunch.com/2017/10/04/announcing-the-2017-update-to-the-crunchbase-women-in-venture-report/.

9   Meisler, Laurie, Mira Rojanasakul, and Jeremy Scott Diamond. "Who Gets Venture Capital Funding?" Bloomberg.com. May 25, 2016. https://www.bloomberg.com/graphics/2016-who-gets-vc-funding/.

10 "First Round 10 Year Project." First Round 10 Year Project. http://10years.firstround.com/.

11 Brush, Candida G. *Growth-Oriented Women Entrepreneurs and Their Businesses: A Global Research Perspective.* Cheltenham: Edward Elgar Publishing, 2006.

12 "How the 'World's Bravest Orchestra' Found Harmony Amid Conflict." Blue Ocean Strategy. January 30, 2018. https://www.blueoceanstrategy.com/blog/the-bravest-orchestra-in-the-world/.

CHAPTER 2

13 Elmore, Kristen C., and Myra Luna-Lucero. "Light Bulbs or Seeds? How Metaphors for Ideas Influence Judgments About Genius." *Social Psychological and Personality* Science 8, no. 2 (2016): 200-08. doi:10.1177/1948550616667611.

CHAPTER 3

14 Busis, Hillary. "In Netflix's *Girlboss*, The Empress Has No Clothes." HWD. May 26, 2017. https://www.vanityfair.com/hollywood/2017/04/girlboss-netflix-sophia-amoruso-nasty-gal-review.

15 Bell, D. A., & White, S. S. (2014). *Gender Diversity in Silicon Valley A Comparison of Silicon Valley Public Companies and Large Public Companies*(Rep.). Fenwick & West LLP.

16 Quinn, Diane M., and Steven J. Spencer. "The Interference of Stereotype Threat with Women's Generation of Mathematical Problem-Solving Strategies." *Journal of Social Issues* 57, no. 1 (2001): 55-71. doi:10.1111/0022-4537.00201.

17 Tinkler, Justine E., Kjersten Bunker Whittington, Manwai C. Ku, and Andrea Rees Davies. "Gender and Venture Capital Decision-Making: The Effects of Technical Background and Social Capital on Entrepreneurial Evaluations." *Social Science Research* 51 (2015): 1-16. doi:10.1016/j.ssresearch.2014.12.008.

18 Zarya, Valentina. "Female Founders Got 2% of Venture Capital Dollars in 2017." *Fortune.* January 31st, 2018. http://fortune.com/2018/01/31/female-founders-venture-capital-2017/.

19 Özkazanç-Pan, Banu, and Paolo Gaudiano. "VC Decision Making, Networks, and Geographies." Lecture, December 4, 2017.

20 *The 2016 State of Women-Owned Businesses Report.* Report. April 2016. http://www.womenable.com/content/userfiles/2016_State_of_Women-Owned_Businesses_Executive_Report.pdf.

CHAPTER 4

21 Schwartz, David Joseph. *The Magic of Thinking Big.* New York: Simon & Schuster, 1987.

22 Timmons, Jeffry A. *New Venture Creation: Entrepreneurship for the 21st Century.* Boston: Irwin/McGraw-Hill, 1999.

23 "Strength Training Using Motor Imagery." Psychology Today. https://www.psychologytoday.com/us/blog/body-sense/201109/strength-training-using-motor-imagery.

24 Sotomayor, Sonia. My Beloved World. New York: Alfred A. Knopf, 2016.

CHAPTER 5

25 Lehrer, Jonah. *Imagine: How Creativity Works*. Houghton Mifflin Harcourt, 2012.

26 Staff, NPR, Robert Siegel, and Jonah Lehrer. "'How Creativity Works': It's All in Your Imagination." NPR. March 19, 2012. https://www.npr.org/2012/03/19/148777350/ how-creativity-works-its-all-in-your-imagination.

27 "Invention of VELCRO® Brand Hook and Loop." Hook and Loop. https://hookandloop.com/invention-velcro-brand.

28 "Slinky." Slinky | National Toy Hall of Fame. http://www. toyhalloffame.org/toys/slinky.

29 "The History of the Ice Cream Cone." International Dairy Foods Association. http://www.idfa.org/news-views/ media-kits/ice-cream/the-history-of-the-ice-cream-cone.

30 History of the Chocolate Chip Cookie. http://iml.jou.ufl.edu/ projects/fall09/saval_j/history.html.

31 "The Invention of Coca-Cola: Birth of a Refreshing Idea." The Coca-Cola Company. January 01, 2012. https://www.coca-colacompany.com/stories/ the-chronicle-of-coca-cola-birth-of-a-refreshing-idea.

32 Pope, Shelby. "How an Eleven-Year-Old Boy Invented the Popsicle." NPR. July 22, 2015. https:// www.npr.org/sections/thesalt/2015/07/22/425294957/ how-an-11-year-old-boy-invented-the-popsicle.

33 McQuaid, John. "The First Potato Chip." *The Atlantic*. December 28, 2014. https://www.theatlantic.com/magazine/ archive/2015/01/the-first-potato-chip/383501/.

34   The Editors of Publications International, Ltd. "9 Things
      Invented or Discovered by Accident." HowStuffWorks
      Science. March 08, 2018. https://science.howstuffworks.com/
      innovation/scientific-experiments/9-things-invented-or-dis-
      covered-by-accident1.htm.

CHAPTER 6

35   Hoomans, Joel. "35,000 Decisions: The Great Choices of
      Strategic Leaders." *Leading Edge Journal*. https://go.roberts.
      edu/leadingedge/the-great-choices-of-strategic-leaders.

CHAPTER 7

36   Dean van Leeuwen. "Competitive Advantage in the
      Connection Economy." Dean Van Leeuwen. July 7,
      2014. https://www.deanvanleeuwen-members.com/
      competitive-advantage-in-the-connection-economy/.

37   SAPPHIRE NOW. "Seth Godin and the Connection
      Revolution." YouTube. June 12, 2013. https://www.youtube.
      com/watch?v=sKXZgTzEyWY.

38   Langer, Ellen J., Arthur Blank, and Benzion Chanowitz. "The
      Mindlessness of Ostensibly Thoughtful Action: The Role of
      "placebic" Information in Interpersonal Interaction." *Journal
      of Personality and Social Psychology* 36, no. 6 (1978): 635-42.
      doi:10.1037//0022-3514.36.6.635.

39   "Project Entrepreneur #theTools Episode 52: Launch, Test,
      Then Raise: How to Bring Your Idea to Market." Interview.
      January 26, 2018.

CHAPTER 8

40 Christensen, Clay. "The "Jobs to Be Done" Theory
of Innovation." Harvard Business Review. August
31, 2017. https://hbr.org/ideacast/2016/12/
the-jobs-to-be-done-theory-of-innovation.

41 "Project Entrepreneur #theTools Podcast, Episode 55:
Metrics That Matter." Interview. February 16, 2018.

CHAPTER 9

42 Huertas, Jason. "My Startup Failed." UC Berkeley
Sutardja Center. March 30, 2015. https://scet.berkeley.edu/
my-startup-failed/.

43 Kenny, Case. "This Healthy Side Project Made
Her Millions... Accidentally." PRSUIT. March
27, 2018. https://prsuit.com/view-from-the-top/
side-project-made-millions-accidentally/.

CHAPTER 11

44 Roberts, Michael J., and Jim Sharpe. "Eric Weston." Harvard
Business School Case 813-045, July 2012. (Revised April 2013.)

45 Charness, Gary, and Uri Gneezy. "Strong Evidence for
Gender Differences in Risk Taking." *Journal of Economic
Behavior & Organization* 83, no. 1 (2012): 50-58. doi:10.1016/j.
jebo.2011.06.007.

46 Jianakoplos, Nancy Ammon, and Alexandra Bernasek. "Are
Women More Risk Averse?" *Economic Inquiry* 36, no. 4
(1998): 620-30. doi:10.1111/j.1465-7295.1998.tb01740.x.

47 Sarin, Rakesh, and Alice Wieland. "Risk Aversion for Decisions under Uncertainty: Are There Gender Differences?" *Journal of Behavioral and Experimental Economics* 60 (2016): 1-8. doi:10.1016/j.socec.2015.10.007.

48 Santos, Ricardo Dos. "Effectuation—The Best Theory of Entrepreneurship You Actually Follow, Whether You've Heard of It or Not." Necrophone. October 20, 2015. https://necrophone.com/2014/01/20/effectuation-the-best-theory-of-entrepreneurship-you-actually-follow-whether-youve-heard-of-it-or-not/.

CHAPTER 12

49 Gilbert, Elizabeth. *Big Magic: Creative Living beyond Fear.*

50 Green, Carrie. TEDxManchester: Programming Your Mind for Success. Speech.

51 Eisenmann, Thomas R., Michael Pao, and Lauren Barley. "Dropbox: 'It Just Works.'" Harvard Business School Case 811-065, January 2011. (Revised October 2014.)

CHAPTER 13

52 "The Top 20 Reasons Startups Fail." CB Insights Research. February 02, 2018. https://www.cbinsights.com/research/startup-failure-reasons-top/.

53 Gilbert, Elizabeth. *Big Magic: Creative Living beyond Fear.*

CHAPTER 14

54 Fernandez-Mateo, Isabel, Raina Brands. "Women Are Less
    Likely to Apply for Executive Roles If They've Been Rejected
    Before." Harvard Business Review. March 07, 2018. https://
    hbr.org/2017/02/women-are-less-likely-to-apply-for-execu-
    tive-roles-if-theyve-been-rejected-before.

55 Garcia, Julio, and Geoffrey L. Cohen. "Identity, Belonging,
    and Achievement." *Current Directions in Psychological
    Science,* 2008.

56 Sandberg, Sheryl. *Lean In: Women, Work, and the Will to
    Lead.* New York: Alfred A. Knopf, 2013.

57 Amoruso, Sophia. *#Girlboss.* Penguin Books Limited, 2015.

58 Godin, Seth. "30 Days of Genius: Seth Godin." CreativeLive.
    https://www.creativelive.com/30-days-of-genius/
    seth-godin?utm_source=creativeLIVE&utm_medi-
    um=blog&utm_campaign=business-money_seth-go-
    din&utm_content=text_link.

59 Kaminski, Jack. "Seth Godin on the Connection Economy: A
    Must-Read for Startup Entrepreneurs." LinkedIn. February
    04, 2016. https://www.linkedin.com/pulse/seth-godin-con-
    nection-economy-must-read-startup-jack-kaminski/.

CONCLUSION

60 Cuddy, Amy Joy Casselberry. *Presence: Bringing Your Boldest
    Self to Your Biggest Challenges.* New York: Back Bay Books,
    2018.

Made in the USA
Monee, IL
19 January 2021